Taurus

The Ultimate Guide to an Amazing Zodiac Sign in Astrology

© Copyright 2021

The content contained within this book may not be reproduced, duplicated or transmitted without direct written permission from the author or the publisher.

Under no circumstances will any blame or legal responsibility be held against the publisher, or author, for any damages, reparation, or monetary loss due to the information contained within this book, either directly or indirectly.

Legal Notice:

This book is copyright protected. It is only for personal use. You cannot amend, distribute, sell, use, quote or paraphrase any part, or the content within this book, without the consent of the author or publisher.

Disclaimer Notice:

Please note the information contained within this document is for educational and entertainment purposes only. All effort has been executed to present accurate, up to date, reliable, complete information. No warranties of any kind are declared or implied. Readers acknowledge that the author is not engaging in the rendering of legal, financial, medical or professional advice. The content within this book has been derived from various sources. Please consult a licensed professional before attempting any techniques outlined in this book.

By reading this document, the reader agrees that under no circumstances is the author responsible for any losses, direct or indirect, that are incurred as a result of the use of information contained within this document, including, but not limited to, errors, omissions, or inaccuracies.

Your Free Gift (only available for a limited time)

Thanks for getting this book! If you want to learn more about various spirituality topics, then join Mari Silva's community and get a free guided meditation MP3 for awakening your third eye. This guided meditation mp3 is designed to open and strengthen ones third eye so you can experience a higher state of consciousness. Simply visit the link below the image to get started.

https://spiritualityspot.com/meditation

Contents

INTRODUCTION 1
CHAPTER 1: INTRODUCTION TO TAURUS 4
    THE TRAITS OF A TAURUS 4
    THE TAURUS CONSTELLATION 10
    THE TAURUS HISTORY 10
    THE BULL SYMBOL 12
    RULING PLANET: VENUS 13
    THE SECOND HOUSE OF POSSESSIONS 13
    TAURUS GEMSTONE AND COLOR 14
    MANTRA AND PURPOSE 14
    THE TAURUS MAN 14
    THE TAURUS WOMAN 15
    THE TAURUS AT WORK 16
    THE TAURUS WITH MONEY 16
    THE TAURUS WITH FRIENDS 17
    THE TAURUS AT HOME 17
CHAPTER 2: TAURUS STRENGTHS 18
    KEY STRENGTHS AND THE SCIENCE BEHIND THEM 18
    SIMILARITIES WITH OTHER SIGNS 22
    COMPATIBILITY WITH OTHER SIGNS 23
    SPOTTING THE STRENGTHS IN OTHERS 24

SPOTTING YOUR TRAITS 25
STRENGTH MYTHS 26
WHEN DOES A TAURUS REALLY SHINE? 27
WHAT A TAURUS NEEDS TO EXCEL 27
CHAPTER 3: TAURUS WEAKNESSES 29
HOW TO OVERCOME THE FEAR OF CHANGE 35
CUSP TAURUS 39
WHAT TO AVOID AS A TAURUS 40
CHAPTER 4: THE TAURUS CHILD 42
CHARACTERISTICS 42
TAURUS CHILDREN AT HOME 43
TAURUS CHILDREN AT SCHOOL 44
TAURUS BOY TRAITS 45
TAURUS GIRL TRAITS 46
HOBBIES AND INTERESTS 46
STABILITY AND ROUTINE 47
EXPLORING THE SENSES 48
EMOTIONAL STABILITY 49
STAYING ACTIVE OUTDOORS 49
PHYSICAL TRAITS 50
ARTISTIC SKILLS 50
BEST TOYS FOR TAURUS CHILDREN 51
THE BEST BOOKS FOR TAURUS CHILDREN 51
BEST ACTIVITIES FOR TAURUS CHILDREN 52
PARENTING TIPS 52
CHAPTER 5: TAURUS IN LOVE 55
WHAT THEY LOOK FOR IN A RELATIONSHIP 55
WHY THEY ARE GREAT LOVERS 56
TURN-ONS AND TURN-OFFS 59
BEST MATCHES 59
WORST MATCHES 62
LOVING A TAURUS WOMAN 63
LOVING A TAURUS MAN 64
ATTRACTING A TAURUS 64

- SIGNS A TAURUS IS INTERESTED 65
- PERFECT DATE IDEAS 65

CHAPTER 6: TAURUS AT WORK 67
- BEST CAREER CHOICES FOR THE TAURUS 67
- WORST CAREER CHOICES FOR THE TAURUS 71
- WHERE DOES THE TAURUS FIT IN AN OFFICE SETTING? 72
- OBSTACLES AT WORK 73
- TAURUS AS A COWORKER OR EMPLOYEE 73
- TAURUS AS A BOSS OR GROUP LEADER 74
- TIPS FOR A FULFILLING WORK LIFE 76

CHAPTER 7: THE SOCIAL TAURUS 80
- TAURUS FRIENDSHIPS 80
- TAURUS FRIENDSHIP GRID WITH THE OTHER 11 ZODIACS 81
- SIGNS THAT DON'T GET ALONG WITH TAURUS 86
- SIGNS THAT GET ALONG WITH TAURUS 87
- TAURUS AT A PARTY: SOCIAL LIFE 88
- WHY DOES A TAURUS MAKE A GREAT FRIEND? 89
- HOW TO FOSTER A TAURUS FRIENDSHIP 90
- APPRECIATING YOURSELF AS A TAURUS 93

CONCLUSION 95
HERE'S ANOTHER BOOK BY MARI SILVA THAT YOU MIGHT LIKE 97
YOUR FREE GIFT (ONLY AVAILABLE FOR A LIMITED TIME) 98
REFERENCES 99

Introduction

The Taurus is one of the earliest zodiac signs, and it's believed to have originated from actual bull worshipping in ancient Mesopotamians, often called "The Great Bull of Heaven." If you aren't familiar with astrology, you will want to read the first chapter of this book carefully, to get a thorough understanding of the parameters that govern the world of zodiac signs. From symbols to planets, the world of zodiac signs is much bigger than you may think.

Taurus people are known for their ability to put up a fight if push comes to shove. Taurus' stubborn nature makes for a very stubborn worker who will always get the job done. Giving up is a fate they seriously despise. The confidence a Taurus has is based in reality, and it's deeply grounded in their belief in themselves. The aura of stability surrounding Taurus people is a great asset in climbing up the corporate ladder and acing the interview.

You will be hard-pressed to find an elegant party that is not hosted by a Taurus. While some signs may find them a bit too formal when it comes to planning parties, a Taurus host knows what they are doing down to the most minute details for hosting events. It's hard to shake off the perfectionism and organization traits of a Taurus regarding any project they do. You will even find them hanging out by the DJ, trying to help with the music choice.

Zodiac signs are often contrasted together by the comparison of weaknesses and strength; not everyone enjoys the same cup of tea. You can always know a Taurus by observing their thought process. It's no wonder why everyone seeks the advice of a Taurus because of how logical and sound it is, built upon facts and realistic perspectives. The more serious the situation is, the more valuable you will find the advice of a Taurus. A Taurus knows how to inject a dose of common sense at the right time, helping others become more grounded in reality and centered. This book will detail the traits that make Taurus a logical thinker and a problem solver.

The generosity of a Taurus is always apparent to both strangers and loved ones. A Taurus has no problems giving themselves to those who they love, preferring to put others before themselves any given day. They hardly play any games and always go for a direct and straightforward approach to gain the trust of the surrounding people. Organization, kindness, understanding, and patience are all popular points of strength that a Taurus has.

A strong zodiac sign comes with its own vulnerabilities. There is no such thing as a perfect sign without any weakness, especially when you consider that the signs complement each other. Taurus people are on the jealous side because of how much work they put into relationships. They may not be the most active people when they don't have serious work to do, preferring to relax instead of doing a fun activity. Some may say a Taurus can easily become possessive with people and objects when things get out of hand.

If you are the lucky parent of a Taurus child, you might be in for quite the ride. Many people are under the wrong impression that Taureans are unstable and angry, but you will be surprised to learn how fun and sensitive they are. Understanding your child's ticks and how they develop a strong personality as a Taurus is important. A Taurus child will happily learn, but their stubbornness may give you a hard time in certain situations. Raising a Taurus child will be referred to later in this book, as you become more familiar with the zodiac sign's personality traits and specifics.

If you are a Taurus, you probably remember how you stuck to your favorite toys and games once you found something you like. You may even remember getting a lot of scolding from your parents because of some ill-tempered destructive sessions. Knowing a young Taurus can help you raise a child and get in touch with your inner child to solve complicated problems deep-rooted in the past.

If you are a Taurus looking for love or receiving love from a Taurus, you may find the compatibility chart in the later chapters useful. Knowing which zodiac signs sync well with a Taurus can help save you a lot of trouble at the beginning and even help solve problems later. As you follow a Taurus teen's love life, you can understand what they find attractive. From the first relationships to the longest ones, a Taurus's traits are dominant and consistent, which should help to know if you are in a relationship with one.

As you continue reading this book, you will learn how to navigate the ups and downs of life with a Taurus. If you happen to be a member of this mighty zodiac sign, you will learn how you can sustain a healthy relationship or repair a damaged one. Tips and hacks related to a Taurus will be presented in a manner that allows you to take quick action and reflect freely on the points you need to highlight.

As you reach the later chapters in this book, you will have acquired some serious insight into how the Taurus mind works. Research is important, but you will want to make sure that you turn knowledge into action. The later chapters focus on helping the Taurus or their friends better understand such a complex zodiac sign. This will also greatly reflect on the career paths that a Taurus should excel and other paths that may not interest them in the long run. The more you learn about the Taurus, the more interested you will be in its infinite potential. You can always read the chapters independently if you'd like to focus on a certain key aspect related to this zodiac sign.

Chapter 1: Introduction to Taurus

As it falls in the middle of spring, Taurus embraces all those born between April 21 and May 21. It comes second in the 12 Zodiac signs, right after Aries, and the Bull symbol represents it. Out of the four Zodiac elements, the Taurus shares the Earth element with the Virgos and Capricorns. These Earth elements are known for their practicality, stoicism, determination, ambitiousness, and love of worldly pleasures.

It's no wonder that Taureans love worldly pleasures in whatever form they take; after all, the planet Venus rules them. It's only fair that they take after her beauty, hedonism, artistry, and passion for pursuing luxury and comfort. If you're curious about how this divine ruler has shaped the Taurus sign, you're in for a treat. Let's get started!

The Traits of a Taurus

If you're a Taurean, then you've probably realized that you can sometimes be a little too stubborn. But if you have a Taurean in your circle of friends or family, then you know that you can't go wrong with keeping a Taurean around. Taureans are loyal and honest to a fault - and that's how you know they will always have your back. They're also intelligent, dedicated, and hardworking. They're generally gentle, but they'll be fierce if they must be - they just really hate being pushed around. If you're wondering where a Taurean is, you should probably visit their home. There are few things they love more than the comfort of their own homes.

With such an intriguing collection of traits, let's get an overview of everything that makes a Taurean who they are.

Taurus Strengths

It's quite common for Taureans to be described using the following words:

- Rational
- Grounded
- Perseverant
- Aesthetic
- Patient
- Sensuous
- Chilled
- Responsible
- Reliable
- Stoic
- Practical
- Devoted
- Honest

Owing to their well-grounded, practical, and realistic nature, they're able to rationalize every situation and keep their emotions in check. This rational mindset makes them able to push through their way in life, achieving whatever they've set their minds to. Besides their unparalleled love for luxury and pleasure, they are usually determined to pull ahead of everyone else to enjoy life as it's supposed to be lived: a lifestyle for the rich and fancy. If one motto described their lifestyle, then it would undoubtedly be "Work Hard, Play Harder."

If there's one thing they value, it's honesty above all else - so expect a severe reaction if you try to pull a fast one on a Taurus. Not only will they be one step ahead of you, but they'll also call you out on your dishonesty and lose trust in you.

Taurus Challenges

There's always a challenging trait that comes with their strengths. After all, strengths and challenges are two sides of the same coin. Here's what the other side of a Taurean's coin would say:

- Obsessive
- Fussy
- Stubborn
- Greedy
- Uncompromising
- Possessive

Too much determination can turn into an obsession, which is popular with Taureans. This obsession can go either way: a work perfectionist or a pleasure-seeking procrastinator. It's usually a combination of both, which is quite a paradox.

It's only natural for Taureans to be stubborn. After all, they make sure to rationalize everything and think ten steps ahead of everyone else before taking any action. This level-headedness and foresight often lead them to trust in their opinion and judgment above others, making others think of them as stubborn. Despite their foresight, sometimes they can fail to see the bigger picture due to this stubbornness, making trial and error the only way to change their perspectives.

With their lifestyle, Taureans are not very fond of change. They will have absolutely no problem following the same routine for years without feeling there's anything wrong with it. But they will find facing sudden changes wrong, and they will fuss over everything and how things should be the way they expected it to be. Did we mention they hate surprises? Because they do. They aren't afraid of voicing their opinions either, even if it's in straight-on challenging authorities.

Taurus Likes

Following the footsteps of their divine ruler, Venus, Taureans love pleasure. They're sensuous, tactile, and like comfort. This makes the list of their likes and interests include the following and more:

- Luxury
- Comfort
- Music
- Romance
- Cooking
- Gardening
- Working with Hands
- Fancy Lifestyle

Taurus Dislikes

But you can expect a Taurean to steer away from any situations resulting in:

- Unexpected Changes
- Drama and Complications
- Insecurity
- Synthetic Material

The Fixed Quality

With Zodiac signs, many factors affect their traits. The sign's element plays a significant role, and we'll know how Earth affects the Taurus. Besides the element, each sign also has its own modality.

Technically, the modality is like the operating mode of the sign. It's how the sign expresses itself and sets itself apart from other fellow signs. There are three modalities: cardinal, fixed, or mutable. A cardinal quality marks the start of the season, and its signs are often described as leaders, traditional, rational, aggressive, and overly cautious. A fixed quality falls in the middle of the season, and fixed signs are considered stable, persistent, reliable, stubborn, and resistant to change. A mutable quality falls at the end of the season or in-between seasonal changes. Mutable signs are flexible, adaptable, versatile, restless, and unpredictable.

Out of these modalities, the Taurus shares the fixed quality with Aquarius, Leo, and Scorpio. Falling in the middle of the season, the Taurus represents stability and consistency. They'll fight anything that poses any danger, no matter how remotely, to their sense of stability and security. Their sense of security is built on the comfort of the known and familiar. When you think about it, these Taurean traits are what you need the most after facing a big bang (read cardinal signs) and before looking for a new adventure (read mutable signs), and that's what makes Taureans the anchor of Zodiac signs.

The Earth Element

Not only is Taurus a fixed sign, but it also belongs to the Earth element. That makes it the most static of all the 12 Zodiac signs with a resistance to change. While some might describe this as stubbornness, Taurus remains constant in all of its glory for a valid reason.

Taurus falls in the middle of spring, right where life invites you to enjoy its harvest and luxury. It represents life's pleasures and comfort, the physical body, and the food we eat. It doesn't change because that's what we need at this time of the year; it's there to influence all the other signs to be inspired by life and what it offers and make use of each moment. After all, the Earth element is the essence and core of all the other elements and their most solid foundation. It's there to help them achieve all materialistic goals, purposes, and desires.

When looking at Virgo, Capricorn, and Taurus, one can easily see how they excel at work and simultaneously make the most out of life's pleasures. They teach us how to manage our finances and reach ultimate heights - not only are they're hardworking and persevering, but they also follow a practical lifestyle that steers away from drama and unnecessary emotional complications.

It's clear that these traits help anyone associated with the Earth element reach greater heights, but the path they take may be too boring for the other elements. Earth signs can follow the same routine for years, having found their sense of peace in the familiar. They often dread any changes that will throw their lives right out of proportion and turn it upside down. They will prefer to settle for a life where they don't feel happy or appreciated enough, emotionally, intellectually, or financially, just to maintain the sense of security they've created for themselves.

Since one of the biggest challenges for any Earth sign, especially the Taurus, is dealing with sudden change, it creates a lack of compatibility with the Air element. Signs associated with the Air element are the fastest and most unpredictable, but that's also why Taurus needs the Air elements to grow and prosper. The best way to balance the Earth element, especially when they're stiff in their ways, is to adopt the Air's mindset.

To find balance, an Earthling would have to integrate new activities into their routine. They'll need to build a habit of seeking new coffee shops, going for a morning walk, socializing in new networks, and dynamic exercises that get their bodies moving. Dance lessons, stretching classes, and modern music are usually good places for a Taurus to start.

While a Taurean is conditioned to questioning everything, they do and second-guessing every new activity they pick up, they can ease their overthinking by creating a more meaningful sense of purpose for all the changes they adopt. By connecting this purpose and getting in touch with their emotions and rational mindset, they'll be able to stop regretting these actions.

The Taurus Constellation

The Taurus constellation has been discovered from 5000 to 1700 BC - before we were even alerted to the Aries' sign. It's been linked to cave paintings dating around 1500 BC. Still, there wasn't a definitive sign describing the Taurus until Babylonian astronomy came around and dedicated the Bull symbol. It's also been known as the Bull of Heaven or The Bull in Front.

The constellation hosts two open clusters: the Pleiades and Hyades, which extend through the Taurus constellation until the beginning of Gemini. The Taurus zodiac signs aligned to the Taurus constellation right until Equinox's precession, which changes its positioning. As of now, Taurus holds the place of the second 30 degrees of the Zodiac circle, right after Aries. While Aries represents the beginning of life and spring, Taurus sustains what Aries has started and holds life in all of its full bloom.

The Taurus History

Being one of the oldest constellations to have been discovered, not surprisingly, to find many myths and history linked to Taurus. The Bull symbol had been adopted in various mythologies due to its essential role in the agricultural calendar. You'll find myths and tales about the Taurus Bull in ancient Babylon, Egypt, Sumer, Assyria, Akkad, Rome, and Greek.

You may be familiar with the Taurus in the Epic of Gilgamesh, where the Goddess Ishtar sent Taurus to assassinate Gilgamesh as a punishment for his advances on her. You might have also heard about the Sumerian Goddess of sexual pleasure, fertility, and warfare, Innana, where she had been closely associated with Taurus, but if we went into the most infamous myths surrounding the Taurus, we won't have to go any further than ancient Greek mythology.

There are primarily two significant stories about Taurus in ancient Greek mythology, both of which are associated with Zeus, the king of all gods. The first myth was a story of false facades, where Zeus disguised himself as a white bull to seduce the legendary Phoenician princess, Europa. It wasn't long until Europa noticed Zeus, disguised as a bull kneeling in front of her, and fell in love with his charm and meekness. That's when she decided to hitch a ride on his back, where he traveled with her across the water to Crete, where she gave birth to three of his children. The story didn't end with a happily ever after - at least, the happily ever after wasn't with Zeus. Europa then escaped and married Asterion, the king of Crete, and her sons inherited the throne after him.

The second myth sheds light on the infidelity of Zeus to his wife Hera, where he had an affair with Io, her priestess. Hera was soon to discover the affair, and that's when she executed her revenge. She cursed Io into a cow that would forever be stung by a gadfly, forcing her to live a life void of settling and comfort. Eventually, Io sought refuge in Egypt, where Zeus restored her original form. Later, she gave birth to his son, who ruled over Egypt after Zeus and a daughter.

These myths build a close correlation with the Taurean man's personality. They tell the story of a powerful and unparalleled man, taking us into the details of his journey as he pursues love, passion, sexual endeavors, and earthly pleasures. They show how even the most influential man will put on a false facade to seduce his love interest and then abduct them on a journey across the world.

They also show how the worse traits can get the better of a Taurean when the planets in this sign are being challenged regarding their dignity and principles. When that happens, the worse side of the traits can take over, giving way to adultery and infidelity, where a married man can have an affair even with his wife's sisters and closest friends.

In short, the myths about Taurus paint a vivid picture of a wandering bull faced to deal with the consequences of his actions. They're someone who had betrayed the closest of friends and the most sacred of relationships, after which they've lost it all. They're forced to wander the Earth's distance looking for what they once had and ruined, trying to find something similar in the process. Little do they know that the only way they can get this love back is by making structural changes in their perceptions and beliefs - which is the most challenging task a Taurean can ever be asked to do.

The Bull Symbol

Taurus is represented by the Bull symbol, specifically, the face and horns of a bull. The origin of the image is assumed to have started with ancient paintings in a cave dating to 1500 BC, but the more definitive theory links the bull to the shape of the Taurus constellation. Regardless of the origin, the Taurus Bull is strongly linked to fertility, growth, and peace, correlating with the beginning of spring and the blooming of life. It's during this season that nature bestows upon us the most benefits and plentiful harvests.

Looking at the Bull in its daily life, it becomes clear how accurate its representation of Taureans is. You'll always find the bull relaxing in nature, surrounded by peace, quiet, relaxing aromas, and lush flavors. If that's not the best description of a Taurus in their natural habitat, we don't know what is.

Ruling Planet: Venus

The Divine Venus rules Taurus. She's represented by a symbol of a circle, indicating the divine spirit above a cross, referring to practicality and physical matter. The symbol speaks volumes to the necessity of bringing the divine to earth; to integrate art and beauty to the materialistic and worldly desires.

Venus is the planet of pleasure, love, sex, fertility, prosperity, desire, beauty, artistry, creativity, satisfaction, and gratitude when it comes to traits. She's not dissimilar to Aphrodite, the Greek Goddess. This combination of tender traits makes a Taurean excel at whatever they do, never forgetting to leave his or her artistic and creative touch in his or her masterpieces. That's why they make great cooks, lovers, artists, and gardeners.

These traits also make them the most loyal and supportive of friends. They appreciate honesty above all else, but they have little tolerance for conflicts, criticism, and emotional blackmail. This combination of traits makes them careful to let people into their lives. Although, when they do, they expect loved ones and rely on them, on an emotional level. Some people might even describe them as needy, obsessive, and possessive. Despite that, they still have the rational side that allows them to see reason and have sound opinions in conflicts and chaotic encounters.

The Second House of Possessions

According to the Twelve-Letter Alphabet of modern astrology, there are twelve houses in the birth chart. Each Zodiac sign rules over its corresponding house, which makes Taurus the ruler of the second house. If the second house is known at all, it's known for its possessions, personal wealth, and security. The house aligns perfectly with the Taureans' love for earthly pursuits and worldly pleasures.

If we go back in time and explore classical astrology, we'd find that Venus had a high affinity to the fifth house. In Venus' words, she found joy in exploring the creativity, sexuality, and pleasure that came in the birth chart of the fifth house. The fifth house was also known for another trait and is popularly described as the house of good fortune. That explains why Venus is often related to good luck, prosperity, fertility, and sexual desires.

Taurus Gemstone and Color

Not surprisingly, the gemstone or birthstone of Taurus is Emerald. The green of the birthstone is the best representation of a Taurean's nature, the prosperity, and the blooming of fields. It's also the color of wealth, something we've learned that Taureans are especially fond of. Taurus also responds to Rose, Quartz, Sapphire, Amber, Aventurine, and Garnet. These birthstones enhance their emotional, physical, and mental health. Naturally, the lucky color of a Taurus is green, owing to its Emerald birthstone. It also responds well to light pink and white.

Mantra and Purpose

Looking at a Taurean's nature, they get their sense of security from their possessions. They're conservative, preservative, and stable thanks to the mantra playing in their head with the words "I Have." Repeating it gives them a sense of purpose in their endeavors and encourages them to build structure, reliability, and stability in their lives, relationships, and goals.

The Taurus Man

With the Taurean man, finding another sign of similar strengths will be hard. You'd be hard-pressed to find someone who is as strong, loyal, trustworthy, honest, tender, patient, and generous as a Taurean man. He'd be willing to go out and beyond to make their partner feel loved and appreciated. Often, he will never pay attention to other flirtations and subtle hints - if not for anything other than he didn't even notice these advances.

He's willing to go all-in into the relationship, which makes him take his time doing so. He'd never rush into the physical aspect of the relationship without making sure he connects on an intellectual level with his partner, and that always takes a lot of time until he feels secure enough to trust their partner. He puts honest communication and transparency above all during this process, as he hates all forms of artificiality.

In return for going all in, he expects the same from their partner. As loving and tender as he can be, he'll be quick to be immovably unforgiving if his partner had betrayed him. But he can get too comfortable in his stoicism after settling in with a partner, owing to his calm and consistent nature. To get a sense of dynamicity in his life and how he can avoid boredom, it will be worthwhile if he takes up sports or outdoor exercises to be more grounded and get ready for action.

The Taurus Woman

Nothing charms a Taurean woman like appealing to her romantic side. You'll need to take your time doing so since she expects you to keep courting her slowly and consistently, even after starting a relationship with her. Just like the Taurean man, she knows that the mental and intellectual connection comes before the sexual bond, so she'll rarely jump into a physical relationship without thinking about the rest of the aspects.

One of the most important things for her is feeling loved and secure, requiring transparent honesty and open communication. False facades and games don't impress her, and she'll be quick to call you out on it. But she appreciates both simple and grand gestures of romance; after all, she takes after her goddess Venus. Once she feels secure enough, she'd give her soul, body, and mind to her partner without a second thought - if he remains faithful to her.

The romantic and tender side of a Taurean woman doesn't make her weak. On the contrary, she remains one of the most practical, reliable, and robust signs of all the zodiacs. She'll be ready to commit to a lifetime with the right partner and plan for a life with children and other blessings, but it takes a lot of patience and effort to unlock all her outstanding traits. She can be distant, preserved, closed, and set in her ways. If she lives with a feeling of guilt, it can eat up her inside and prevent her from ever feeling satisfied.

The Taurus at Work

Taureans love money. They love all forms of luxury, and they know that it doesn't come without working hard and making enough cash to sustain their luxurious lifestyle - so they go all in. You'll find that Taureans are among the most dedicated, capable, creative, practical, and hardworking people in whatever field they work in. Whether they're employees or managers, it won't make a difference because they'll do the job perfectly. They'll quickly establish a routine and focus on the task at hand, regardless of what's happening around them. Perhaps the only downside to their strong work ethics is that there's a fine line between dedication and obsession - something that Taureans often cross readily without noticing. Their obsession with work can turn them into perfectionists who expect everyone to go the extra mile, just like they do. They reward themselves for their hard work by playing and enjoying the luxuries of life even harder.

The Taurus with Money

As someone ruled by the second house of wealth, you'd expect a Taurean to be good with finances - and they won't disappoint. They're able to make do with both small and large salaries, planning their lifestyle according to their financial state. They'll never forget to leave some savings for a rainy day, and they'll consider their responsibilities, retirement saving, and both short and long-term goals.

The Taurus with Friends

Taureans thrive on the sense of stability they make sure they build for themselves. It's common to find a Taurean depending on this sense of peace with their circle of friends either, possibly even managing to maintain all their childhood friendships strong and precious. Once they let you in their life, they'll be some of the most loyal and supportive friends you have. They'll make it a point to keep nurturing your relationship and maintaining a healthy, honest, and pure bond that can last a lifetime. They're the Hufflepuffs of the zodiac signs.

The Taurus at Home

The ultimate form of stability for a Taurean is building a home with their family and living happily ever after. They're people who value family above all else, so you can expect them to show their love, support, and reliability to their parents and siblings from as early on as they can talk and move. As they grow up and take their paths in life, they'll settle with their loved partner and plan for ways to fill their home with laughter and happiness. They'll fill the house with kids and appreciate every second of the day, and they'll never say no to host a gathering of family and friends.

Chapter 2: Taurus Strengths

Having a Taurus in your life can be a blessing in disguise. They are sophisticated characters with more traits than meets the eye. You will need to get to know them to understand what is going on in their minds and how they think. Those born under this zodiac sign are interesting characters with numerous capabilities and strengths. Exploring those strengths can be quite a journey itself. If you were born under this sign with the sun, feel proud and unique, as you will come to learn how worldly your character can be. Here is everything you need to know about Taurus's strengths and how you can identify them in yourself if you're a Taurus or in someone you know.

Key Strengths and the Science Behind Them

Determining a zodiac sign's strengths in astrology is not something that some people just guess or make it up. A whole science behind it makes it easy to spot these positive traits and work on nourishing them if they are not too noticeable. This science is represented through three modalities, and they are basically the way each zodiac sign expresses itself. The modality types are fixed, mutable, and cardinal. With the case of a Taurus, they follow the fixed modality. To understand how Taureans express themselves, it is essential to understand the different modalities and how they work. Each modality has a mix of signs that make up for all the elements, which are Fire, Air, Water, and Earth.

Cardinal

This modality is the oldest one in all the groupings. Its signs are Aries (Fire), Libra (Air), Cancer (Water), and Capricorn (Earth). These characters are adventurous and outgoing. They express themselves loudly and say whatever they think, which is a positive or negative trait depending on the context and the situation. The Cardinal signs like to assert their dominance and leadership wherever they may be.

Fixed

With the fixed modality qualities, the Taurus can be seen shining along with other signs like Leo, Scorpio, and Aquarius. The Fixed signs are steady in their elements, making their strengths visible and noticeable as you get to know them. Their steadiness can often make them seem stubborn, but they are believers and stand for their beliefs no matter what the obstacles are. Taurus is an Earth sign, which makes Taureans even more determined and stable, but do not take no for an answer, and they get what they want in any way possible. They are not exactly revolutionaries or big fans of change, but they do like things happening their way. You will often see Taureans leading steady, fixed lives like their modality, where there is little room for surprises.

Mutable

Looking at the Mutable signs in comparison with other modalities, they are all about the change. Mutable signs are Sagittarius, Pisces, Gemini, and Virgo. Those born under these signs and have the mutable qualities are ever so restless. They always like to be active and, on the move, and they appreciate the change to a great extent. Settling for anything is not their strongest suit, and they can sometimes be a little chaotic. They are great communicators, making it easy for them to form friendships with those with other modality qualities like the Taureans.

Work Capabilities

The Taurus personality is very hardworking and determined. You can see them shine when they are at work or taking on a certain project in their careers. You can easily spot a Taurean in your workplace, as they will show great ambition and tenacity regularly. They can be a little competitive, but that is a good thing, as they will keep everyone around them on their toes and up for the competition. They are likely to become team leaders quickly and early in their careers. Those born under this zodiac sign are like seeds waiting to grow with the right nutrition, especially for succeeding in their fields and careers.

When you think of a Taurus's work capabilities, always think about discipline and punctuality. In specific fields like agriculture or admin management, those born under this sign will be excellent for the job. It is rare to see Taureans not being punctual or missing any details because they were too laid back or unfocused. But they are responsible and precise in their every move.

They can also be some of the most creative artists you have ever come across. Those with a Taurus personality are abstract in their way of thinking. This allows them to create exciting pieces of art and express their thoughts in a unique way you will not see with anyone else born under a different star sign. They are disciplined even in their art, which helps them notice beauty in everything to portray it in their artwork. Their artistic and musical taste is as classy as it comes. Even if they don't practice art themselves, they can still appreciate it when they see it. If you have a Taurus in your inner circle, it will be relatively easy to see how much they are interested and entertained by different artwork.

Since art is not just painting or listening to music, Taureans can excel in other creative fields like construction. This field needs hard-working, pragmatic, and artistic individuals, and it is super easy to find all these traits in a Taurus individual. They will add their sophisticated personal touch likely to change the way any construction work they get their hands on for the better.

Positive Social Aspects

Taureans are not necessarily perceived to be very sociable, but that doesn't mean it's a bad thing. Them being loners at times is a great strength. They are adaptable, and they can do things on their own with no help from anyone. They are human, though, and they still need some form of social interaction. When you get close to a Taurus and become their friend, they will be loyal to you for as long as you show them respect and appreciation. Do not mistake their loyalty for weakness. They will stand by you no matter what you get yourself into, but if you ever take that support for granted, they will not look back to the friendship they had with you twice.

One of the great things about Taureans is that they are also very consistent. They do not like change; you can go for months or even years without speaking to them and come back to find them the same. They are not easily influenced by others or by the world around them. That is why it is almost impossible to find a Taurean who has changed over time or become a different person than what you used to know.

Another great quality that is rare to find in any other sign but easy to spot with any Taurus in your circle is reliability. Whether the Taurean in your life is your friend, partner, or even mentor, you can always count on them to get things done and have your back whenever you need them. You won't have to ask them for anything twice as they will have it in the back of their minds until they can get you what you need or have asked of them. Responsibility is their middle name, and you can always count on them to seize the day.

Taurus with Family

Every family has a rock, someone they can rely on and go to when things go south. If you look closely at all the members of your own family, you will come to notice that the rock of the family is often a Taurus. Family is always the main priority for a Taurus. They do not take household matters lightly and can be protective of their loved ones. They might struggle to show their love for those they care about, but deep down, they would do anything for them, and that makes them powerful characters. They will often show their love to those in their home subtly by preparing special meals or spoiling them with lavish gifts.

Being good with kids is also one of the main qualities of this star sign, as they are funny and understanding. Taureans are perfect fun aunt or uncle material. They will spoil all related kids and shower them with love and attention. If they have children, they are likely to be mini versions of themselves. Whatever they ask for, they will probably get in the end. The main things any kid needs growing up are supportive parents, and a bull character is precisely that. They are overprotective with their children, but they would do anything for them.

Similarities with Other Signs

The qualities and traits of a Taurus are unique but are not that rare. You can easily spot certain positive characteristics like those of other zodiac signs. This can sometimes make it challenging for people to know on the first encounter whether the person in front of them is a Taurus, but by understanding the similarities and slight differences these characters have, you can tell them apart.

Taurus is an Earthly sign, which means the similarities it has with other earthly signs are numerous. Capricorn and Virgo are very grounded signs that share the stability trait with Taurus. They are all big fans of security and balance and might not always like surprises. Not that they won't know what to do if they experience shock or an emergency. Taureans share that trait with Capricorns and Virgos, where they will take charge if any emergency occurs or surprise event and deal with it responsibly and effectively.

In terms of similarities with other signs following other elements like water, air, and fire, Taureans share particular social traits with Sagittarius and Scorpio. With Sagittarius, both zodiac signs love their families more than anything and will do anything for them. They can be great parents and will always prioritize their loved ones over anything else. Scorpios share positive social traits with Taureans, where they are also reliable people who show support to those they care about and are reliable when times get tough.

Taureans share an essential trait with fellow earthly Virgos. They are both sensual signs with a unique, artistic sense that allows them to think creatively and logically. Every step they take is calculated, but they are practical and can adapt to any situation they are put in to be comfortable yet productive. You will not need to take care of these two Earthly signs as they can take good care of themselves and others. Taureans, Virgos, and Capricorns are all committed beings who can get things done with or without anybody's help and will show unmatchable results full of creative thinking and innovation.

Compatibility with Other Signs

Every zodiac sign has its match; it is the people they feel most comfortable around and understood by. With Taurus, they are compatible with fellow earthly signs and other star signs. When it comes to overall compatibility, they can easily get along with Capricorns. They also follow the same modality traits and will find comfort in one another. It is easy for a Taurus to open up when they are around someone they feel comfortable with, and that is something Capricorns can offer them. This trusting relationship helps a Taurus feel more confident in sharing personal experiences and can easily exercise self-expression.

Because Taureans love stability so much and can easily thrive in an environment where they have plenty of experience and people they trust, they might not always get along with signs like Gemini or Aries. These signs are all about change and adventurous surprises, which Taureans might not like much. Yes, they can adapt if they face such a surprise, but they would not appreciate it.

Two Taureans can get along well and understand each other's needs and wants as they have similar experiences in life. Their powerful traits will thrive together in such a relationship, whether it is a romantic or strictly platonic one. Even if the other Taurus in your life is a family member, you will quickly come to notice that being around them is comfortable and reassuring as their way of thinking is the same as yours.

Just because Earth rule Taureans, it does not mean they cannot get along well and share similar traits with other signs and elements. In fact, signs that follow the water element are often a perfect match in a work environment and a home environment. Earth and Water go hand in hand in nature, and that is a similar case to other zodiac signs.

Spotting the Strengths in Others

If you have a Taurus in your life you know and love, then it'll be easy to spot their most formidable characteristics and capabilities. But if you do not know the person that well, then spotting these strengths might be a challenge. but you can find these strengths the more you spend time with them and get to know their back-story. The life experiences a Taurus shares with you can quickly make you realize just how resilient they are and what they can do. Not all Taureans share the same strong and positive traits, and it's rare to find them all in just one person. People are different; you are likely to find a bulk of traits in one person and another set of strengths in another.

You can learn more about a Taurean's positive traits by seeing how they spend their time. If they are into artistic activities, you will understand that their sense of creativity is higher than anything else. If they like spending their time working or laboring, you can find that they thrive on earnest hard work when they are on their own, and they are committed to whatever task they have at hand with nobody else's help. They can have all the strong traits of a bull or just a few. It is up to the surrounding people to discover what they excel at.

Being a Taurus's friend will help you get a better insight as to what their personality is like. They will be a good friend, for sure, but whether their loyalty is their best feature or their reliability, which is what will differ from one Taurus to the other. You can simply ask them what their strongest skills and characteristics are, but it is always more exciting to discover these traits for yourself as you get to know a Taurean.

Spotting Your Traits

If you are a Taurus yourself, learning about your strengths might be a little more challenging than what you would expect. Not everyone knows what he or she is good at and where he or she excels in life. You can have all the right traits and qualities within you and still not know they are there; you might not even know how to utilize them, but it need not be that way forever. Digging deep within yourself and your emotions will help you figure out where you can shine as a Taurus and what fields will be a perfect match for your capabilities.

Start by looking at your hobbies and interests. If there is something that you particularly love doing, even if it is nothing too major, then that might be your strongest suit, and you need to nourish it. For example, if you like doing any form of art in your spare time, then that can be your real calling, and focus on making a career out of it or occupying yourself with your artistic side more often.

Taureans often prefer working alone and having an independent life. That can be an asset within you never knew about. Leading an independent life can help people discover more about themselves and see the full extent of their capabilities. It will help show how responsible a Taurus can be and how well they can take care of themselves on their own.

Strength Myths

People often think that the myths about any zodiac sign are just about their weaknesses or what they cannot do or even who are they are or are not compatible with. But there are a few common myths about a Taurean's strength that can be misleading for those with a Taurus within their network or who were born under the Zodiac sign themselves.

Among the most common myths about Taureans is that they are easygoing and mellow. That is not any far from the truth. They are adaptable beings that make the best of a situation they might find themselves in, whether it was good or bad, but they are not easygoing as that trait is overpowered by them being determined and wanting things to go a certain way, one that gives them comfort and stability.

Another trait that Taureans are often mistaken for is being overly confident. They are confident in themselves and their abilities, but they are not so confident that it makes them irritate to others. You won't have to worry about a Taurus stealing the show or taking all the attention. They like getting things done in peace - drawing no attention to themselves. Of course, they will appreciate it when their efforts are recognized, but they won't go around trying to show them off.

When Does a Taurus Really Shine?

Having character strength is not something that comes and goes, but is something that a person develops and grows over time. There are certain seasons and times when your zodiac sign will shine and come to light. The Taurus season is when a bull's positive traits come out to show obviously. That is from the duration of April 20 to May 20 every year. They will be the most like themselves and can reveal a lot of liveliness and success during that period.

You can also see a Taurus in their element when doing something they love and are passionate about regardless of the season. It could be working in the field of their dreams or spending their time with loyal friends or family members they love and appreciate, which is when all their positive and robust qualities become obvious and come to life.

What a Taurus Needs to Excel

Anyone needs to be placed in the right environment for their most vital abilities to shine. With Taureans, they need to be surrounded by a reliable support system just like themselves to excel in whatever place they are in. These characters like stability and having constants they can go back to whenever they need to. When they find themselves in a comfortable environment and surrounded by a loving network of individuals they are compatible with, you will see them becoming the best version of themselves. Taureans need honest people around them who will tell them all they need to know straightforwardly, sugarcoating no facts. They are pragmatic people who respond well to logic and can handle anything they encounter when they have all the facts.

Taureans are not complicated beings. They are very straightforward thinkers who go through life with a lot of determination and ambition. It is almost impossible to shake a Taurean's faith in anything they believe in. If you treat them right, they can be your best friend and most loyal confidant. Whether you are a Taurus yourself or have a Taurus in your life, you must learn about what makes those born under this sign special and unique. They are loving and kind, and anyone would be lucky to have them in their life.

Chapter 3: Taurus Weaknesses

Like all signs in the zodiac, Taureans have their fair share of shortcomings that need to be addressed. Building on the Taurean's practicality and positive traits we discussed in the earlier chapter, understanding one's 'weaknesses' is an essential tool in understanding how to deal with a Taurus. If you have a Taurean in your life or are one, you know how this can help reach the stability this sign incessantly seeks and thrives for. Unlike other books on the market, you won't just find an explicit list of a Taurus' weaknesses; instead, you will come to understand the why behind every trait.

In this chapter, you will also learn how each weakness can be made them work for you or your Taurean friend or acquaintance instead of against them. This is a book you will want to pull out every time you are ready to go deeper and gain a more profound sense of self. Otherwise, if you are not a Taurean yourself, you will still need this book to know how to best interact with every new Taurus you come across in life. One thing you need to remember, as an avid astrology fan, is that we can't just pool all Taureans together, which is why you will find a separate section dedicated to the weaknesses of Taurean born on the cusp towards the end of this chapter. But for now, let's focus on the Taurus natives:

Stubbornness

There is a good explanation as to why a double-horned bull is the symbol of the Taurus sign. Taureans are stubborn – so incredibly stubborn that it takes a lot to make them even budge to change their minds about something or someone. If you have a Taurean in your inner circle, you know how hard it can be to convince your Taurean friend to see your viewpoint or even meet you in the middle. Taureans don't do "middles," which can make it very challenging for other people to always accept this single-minded approach. Fellow fixed sign peeps like Leos, Scorpios, and Aquarians may find cultivating a harmonious relationship with Taureans challenging, but to Taureans, it's not about being stubborn because they wholeheartedly believe that their way is the right way.

And most of the time, their stubbornness results from their strong aversion to change, as we mentioned earlier in this book. Unless you have an eloquent and well-thought argument, you'll never convince your Taurean husband to invest in a new dryer instead of fixing the one you have for the third time! While it might sound like you're never going to win with the Taureans in your life, there are tricks that you can use to work around this challenging trait.

Do Not Corner Taureans

Like all people, when put in an uncomfortable situation, Taureans will be triggered to activate defense mechanism. To have a smooth relationship with your Taurean spouse or friend, don't take communication in the direction of your word versus theirs; instead, listen to what they have to say first and then add on to their ideas. You may win them over by making them feel that you are on the same side rather than using unnecessary labels like "your idea" vs "my idea."

Maintain Honest and Open Communication

To more easy-going signs, dealing with a bull-headed Taurean can be depleting and consuming. but this shouldn't be an excuse to avoid engaging with your Taurus friends altogether. On the contrary, aim to have an honest and ongoing conversation to gain their trust and encourage them to become more lenient in your relationship.

Give Them Time

For example, rushing your Taurean son to get into the school night routine after having been on long summer vacation will backfire. It will do you both good if you accept that he will need more time before he can get into the new routine. Though, not only should you accept it, you need to show him you understand and that it's ok, and that you are here to support him if/when he needs your help.

These simple changes in perspective can be all that you need to cultivate a more constructive relationship with the Taureans in your life. But what if you are a Taurean yourself? How can you overcome your stubbornness and not let it get in the way? Here are techniques that you should try:

Pause and Think Before You Act

Often, even if you can't openly admit it, like most Taureans, you have this belief you can do things better than others. You also think that whatever others are suggesting, your ideas are probably superior. But this mentality can push your loved ones away because they feel like you don't need nor value their inputs.

An excellent way to work around it is to pause and take a deep breath before you judge someone's idea as good or bad. Teach yourself to listen more and that not everything that happens in front of you needs a reaction. Over time, you will become more accepting and can easily allow others to have their way occasionally. Still, this will need some time before getting used to, but if the intention to change is there, you will eventually see results.

Get to Know People Around You on a Deeper Level

This technique alone can help you immensely with your stubbornness. When you become intentional about getting to know people around you better, you will learn to trust them more and become more willing to embrace their thoughts instead of insisting on yours. Especially if you are still young or starting a new job or moved to a new country, the only way you can become successful in such scenarios is to show your interest and respect towards other people. Don't give your new coworkers a reason to avoid working with you because you are too fixated on having your way all the time. Express interest and curiosity in others and see how this will improve your relationships and make them mutually rewarding.

Get Out of Your Comfort Zone More Often

True, you are a Taurean that hates change, but you're also persistent by nature. If you set your mind to becoming less stubborn, you will do whatever it takes to make it happen. One of the great ways to do so is to put yourself in situations you would typically try to avoid at all costs. If you aren't big on social gatherings, try to go out more and hang out with people from all walks of life. This way, you will become exposed to various mindsets and backgrounds, which will compel you to become more tolerant. With time, you won't need to enforce your viewpoint over everyone else's.

What's interesting is that your friends and family are likely to start giving you compliments and patting you on the back for becoming more flexible, even if you don't see it yourself yet. But when you give yourself some time and space to experience each of the above, you will feel more comfortable in your relationships and become more accepting of new situations.

Possessiveness

Taureans are possessive creatures, whether it's about people or worldly possessions; they like to claim ownership of what's theirs. With relationships, this trait can be suffocating to their partners. A Taurean's possessive nature is a byproduct of their insecurity and inability to celebrate other people's successes. It either makes them feel less than or insufficient as humans, so they overemphasize ownership. If you are in a relationship with a Taurean, don't take it as a sign of lack of trust; otherwise, you won't be able to continue together. Possessive Taureans can only thrive in relationships where their partners can accept belonging to them and become an extension of themselves.

Besides being possessive with people, Taureans are also possessive with their possessions and they rarely accept having others share their belongings, or their wealth. Being skillful with money, possessive Taureans usually come across as greedy and ungenerous. Even though that's not wrong, that's not usually their intention. If you are having a hard time teaching your daughter born under Taurus about the importance of sharing, or you're dating a Taurean and have trouble enjoying a peaceful relationship, there is a way out. Here are some tips that might help:

Show Compassion

Dismissing possessiveness as an unaccepted trait won't get you far with Taureans, but it will make it even harder for them to trust you, and they may shut you out altogether. A better approach is to show compassion and acknowledge their feelings. For example, you can discuss the recent blowout you had with your jealous boyfriend in a more understanding and loving way. Start by expressing your appreciation for his love and then ask what would make him feel more comfortable moving forward. That you took this tone instead of blaming and pointing fingers will encourage him to relax and show more faith in you.

Involve Your Taurean Friends

Rather than ignoring your Taurean friend, involve them more in your plans. Give them your time and attention so they can feel safe and loosen up a little. When you're going out with other friends, ask them to come along, this way, they'll be sure that you aren't trying to replace them.

Be Possessive

If you can't fight them, join them! That's not to suggest you base your relationship on mutual smothering attention. Instead, you can try to reciprocate your Taurean partner's possessive feelings in a more loving and caring way since it's how they express their love.

As a Taurean, even if you aren't ready to own up to this personality trait, pay attention to the tips below so you can apply them once you are ready:

Self-Analyze

Not to be confused with self-criticize. Self-analyzing is more about getting to know you better and analyzing your underlying insecurities and inhibitions. Pay close attention to what situations trigger your jealousy or possessiveness. Ask yourself the hard questions and dig deep to find the answers. You can also work with a therapist if you believe that your actions are wreaking havoc on your closest relationships. It won't be an easy journey, but it'll be eye opening and eventually comforting.

Always Give Others the Benefit of the Doubt

To you more than others, this is essential to cultivate healthy relationships. Before you jump to conclusions because your boyfriend was late in calling you back, run the million possible scenarios in your head first, then wait for him to call. Not only will this help you calm your mind, but it'll also give your partner the chance to relax and live more authentically without constantly worrying about your possessive behavior.

This trip applies not only to romantic relationships. If you are having a hard time at work delegating to your team members some of your responsibilities, you can follow the same approach. Make yourself believe that your employees want what's best for your company because it reflects on their livelihood. Also remind yourself that doing this job means they already have the needed skills and experience. The more you talk yourself into seeing the good in those around you, the more you'll be able to keep your controlling tendencies in check.

Keep Yourself Busy

As an excelling hard-working Taurus, this shouldn't be a problem for you. Focusing on other things than those that trigger your possessive nature is an easy way to weaken the effects they have on you. Try a new sport or hobby that can keep your mind occupied instead of running wildly when free. It's doubtful that you will turn into a mild-tempered individual who doesn't respond in provocative situations, but you will become more mindful of your actions, and you'll find that you'll do a better job of not hurting the ones you love.

How to Overcome the Fear of Change

Whether it's in their personal or professional lives, Taureans not only despise change, but they also fear it. To Taureans, change is not an idea they can easily entertain, even if their lives depended on it. If you're a Taurean yourself, you know that even the thought of change can be enough to cause you anxiety. This sign likes stability and prefers to live a predictable life where everything goes as planned and expected. To other more flexible signs like Geminis or Leos, Taurus' aversion to change is a huge turnoff, but other insecure signs like the super-sensitive Cancer rely on the 'stable' Taurus to take the lead and keep things steady.

Taurus' fear of change is influenced by their strong belief in structure and always wanting to be in a setup where they can expect what's coming next. This might explain why changing their mind doesn't come easy either, as they don't know how to deal with an unfamiliar outcome. Yet, this quality is usually more sabotaging to Taureans themselves than to those around them. For example, a Taurean in a failing relationship will usually take longer than others before pulling the plug once and for all. Even with their career, although most Taureans are career-driven and successful, it usually takes them a long time to admit that their job isn't a good fit and that they need to find a new one. To learn how you can best deal with the routine enslaved Taureans in your life, you can try these tips.

Taureans Hate Change

You might be coming from a good place wanting to help your Taurean friends open up to life after a bad break up but pushing her into it might do more harm than good. It's better if you can offer her the support and company that she needs until she chooses to move forward herself. You can take her out and go on fun trips together, but you shouldn't be doing more. When under pressure, Taureans can become aggressive, pushing away their loved ones because they don't know how else to react.

Nurture and Encouragement

Raising a change fearing Taurean child can be daunting to any parent. You'll always be worried about them because you know how changing schools or a new teacher can be too much for them to handle, but the best thing you can do is to be there for them. Show them you believe in them and will always have their backs. Besides mouthing the words, let your actions speak for you. Cheer them on from the first row when they play their first soccer match at their new school. With time, you will see that your child will become more willing to cope with change instead of complaining about it like they usually would.

Fear of Change

People born under the Taurus sign are usually realistic, but their fear of change can prevent them from standing back up after falling. Your job as a friend is to help them find the silver lining. Talk to them about the lessons they should learn from a bad experience and then give them the space to make the needed changes to move past it.

A deeper understanding of the reasons behind your fear of change can be just what you need to overcome it. Here are tips that you can try for a little push to make the necessary changes,

1. Grow Your Faith

Most of the time, change is brought upon you when you're least expecting it. The only way you can break free from your fear of change is to have more faith. Trust that everything happens for a reason and that no matter how things go, it'll ultimately be for the greater good. When you train your mind to believe that the universe is working for you and not against you, you will find it easier to accept the idea of change.

2. Commit to Change

While this might sound counter-intuitive, it's an amazing way for a stubborn and persevering Taurean to tip the scales in your favor. They say that the best defense is a good offense in football, and that's exactly what you should do with change. Instead of always being on the receiving end, being someone who doesn't like surprises, take the initiative, and start the change yourself. Try something different every day. These can be as simple as changing your coffee order or taking a new route to your office. These small and simple actions will train your subconscious to accept change as a part of life when done consistently. You will no longer see it as something that you need to avoid wholeheartedly.

3. Tap into Your Practical Nature

Among the 12-star signs of the zodiac, you are by far one of the most practical ones. Tap into your practicality to conquer your irrational fear of change. Starting a new job? Focus on the higher salary and all the status that comes with the new title. Being wealth-driven and someone who appreciates the finer things in life can be enough to make you forget about your fears.

4. Avoiding Change

Yes, you read that, right! Whenever you can, and if it won't set you back in life, you can always choose to avoid change. You shouldn't feel shamed into welcoming change with open hands just so other people don't think of you as another stubborn Taurus. If a particular way of life is working for you and you aren't hurting yourself or anyone else, then decline that overseas job offer and stay put.

5. Laziness

This varies from one person to another, but in general, Taureans are relatively lazier than others. Again, this comes from their need for stability and lack of enthusiasm for experiencing anything new. Laziness is obvious in Taurean children. If you have a Taurean child in the family, you can clearly see they are not the outdoorsy sporty type; they prefer to hang out in peace indoors. But don't despair because there are things that you can do to make them more active.

6. Don't Over Spoil Them

Over-spoiling lazy Taurean kids is a recipe for disaster. With their lazy demeanor, having all their wishes granted will only make them grow into entitled unappreciative adults. Teach your Taurean kid about the importance of working for what they want. For example, if your Taurean daughter has been asking for a new pair of sneakers, give her chores to finish and pay her the money to buy them herself. This way, you will be encouraging her to do something purposeful instead of idly lying around.

7. Be a Good Example

Steady Taureans appreciate consistency. You can't expect them to follow your advice if your actions contradict your talk. The best way to inspire your Taurean friend to get moving is by showing them the active life you lead. Making them understand that it's the right way to live if they want to live a long healthy life will probably urge them to do the same.

If you are a lazy Taurean yourself, you can:

8. Start Small

Doing simple, consistent changes is the only way you can reverse your laziness curse. Instead of deciding on a whim to work out every day, aim for 2-3 days/week, and then add, more as you go.

9. Take Frequent Breaks

Because motivation doesn't come easy to you, schedule infrequent breaks where you can recharge and clear your mind before you get back and finish the tasks at hand.

Cusp Taurus

As promised at the beginning of this chapter, if you are born on the cusp of Taurus, you will find something for you here. Besides the native Taurus qualities, being on the cusp means that either Aries or Gemini influences you, which are the signs adjacent to Taurus.

Aries-Taurus Cusp

Being born on the Aries-Taurus cusp means you were born on the cusp of Power. You are resilient and authoritative, but having this fiery personality often puts you into a lot of trouble because you can't just stop and think. Even though you don't intend to, you tend to offend those around you with your careless ways. This can drive away even your closest friends and family. Though, if you want to make sure you use your powers to your benefit, don't overlook kindness. More than others, your words can use a little-sugar coating to balance out your bluntness. Throw in a smile, and you will be able to avoid alienating the ones that you love without losing yourself in the process.

Taurus-Gemini Cusp

As an individual born on the cusp, you are full of energy and zeal, but you tend to overindulge and rarely know when to stop. Whether it's partying or eating, there's no stopping you. This behavior can take a toll on you mentally and physically and leave you feeling drained. The best way to overcome the imminent burnout is to practice self-control consciously. Have an ongoing conversation with your mind to stop you from devouring the entire bag of chips in one go. Over time, you will be able to keep this destructive behavior in check.

Taureans are highly influential and one of the strongest signs. As you have read in this chapter, their weaknesses mainly emanate from their rigidness and inflexibility. In the following chapters, you will get to see how the above weaknesses influence how Taureans act in other aspects of life, including love, work, and family.

What to Avoid as a Taurus

Naturally, there are some negative traits that a Taurus may have, and they can make life much more difficult if left unchecked. It's easy to become a bit self-absorbed due to the highly focused dynamic that a Taurus maintains. It's crucial to identify behavioral tendencies that are not healthy for you and know how to maneuver yourself into safety.

Self-Indulgence

Getting carried away is one of the bad traits of Taurus people. This can mean that they may over-indulge themselves to guarantee that the fun never stops, which develops a habit of procrastination. Being perfectionists, they can still maintain a great professional path, but they can easily stray away if their ambition is drowned in self-indulgence and hedonism.

Laziness

Even though Taureans are greatly ambitious, they aren't the most active sign. It's always harder for people who value perfectionism to start something due to the fear that it won't turn out as planned. A Taurus should always keep their priorities straight and focus on starting the task quickly instead of being shackled by hesitance. Keeping a distinct line between work and leisure time is very important if you want to maintain a healthy schedule.

Materialism

A sign that is governed by Venus is bound to have a knack for shiny and expensive things. It's common for Taureans to think that life is all about financial success. While financial freedom is great, it's not the only thing in life worth working for. Being flexible and appreciating the little things in life can help Taurus overcome a lot of difficult challenges.

If you are a friend of a Taurus, you will learn a lot of information that can help you with developing better communication with them, in addition to helping them out in a pinch. Not knowing the best traits you have and what you need to develop your character further can be such a huge waste in the case of a Taurus. As mentioned in this book, a Taurus possesses an abundance of outstanding characteristics.

Chapter 4: The Taurus Child

If you are lucky enough to be the parent of a Taurus, then you should count your blessings. Taurean children are among the easiest to bring up and can grow to be unique human beings. By knowing everything there is to know about this sign from an early age, parents will be able to nurture all the right skills their child possesses and help them develop their strengths effectively. Your child's characters will start appearing from early on, even as a baby. Babies born between April 19 and May 20 are like no other newborn. Here is everything you need to know about them as a parent or someone who is expecting a baby Taurus in the family.

Characteristics

Baby Taureans begin their life and approach every action they take differently. They are not like every other kid you will meet. They can be very calm and even shy at times. Parenting Taureans is all about taking into consideration their emotional attributes as well as logical attributes. They won't always express how they feel in words. It can rather be seen in their actions and how they interact with their parents, other family members, or even different people in their social network as kids. Sometimes, you might need to give them their space for them to feel comfortable and be able to find comfort with themselves.

If one of the parents is a Taurus themselves, they might understand their child's needs even more than themselves. Remembering what it was like to be an earthly born kid and how it can sometimes feel like nobody in the world fully understands the way you think or feel can be quite helpful for a parent when it comes to raising their Taurean child. It'll help them relate to personal experiences from the past and understand how their child might think and why they can sometimes behave the way they do.

A Taurus child has a wide range of bold characteristics. They are stubborn, emotional, loving, and warm. They are pretty much born to grow into their roles as family-oriented people. They can have a deep connection to their mothers, but they love everyone in their family just because of the blood ties they share. They are also relatively calm, so they won't be as irritating as some kids might be and are not likely to give you a hard time even if they are upset over anything. Teaching them a lesson won't be difficult since they like to listen and follow the rules. Overall, they are obedient kids who are likely to grow to become successful adults with great potential.

Taurus Children at Home

All children are most comfortable when they are at home, as it is where they have maximum personal space while still being surrounded by loved ones. It is a perfect balance for a Taurus child, and it's the ideal environment to shine. It might not always be comfortable at home with a Taurus kid as they can sometimes become too stubborn, and their parents may lose their patience. When they are set in their ways, the parents need to understand that negotiating logically is the key to resolving arguments in such cases. Of course, with a child, mature logic might not be the way to go. Nonetheless, if you explain all the facts to them and let them in on how you're thinking as a parent, they might just get along with you and become less stubborn.

Parenting is all about learning your child's traits and seeing how you can help them develop their strengths and manage their negative traits into positive ones. If a parent is rational enough at home with their kid, they will become determined individuals rather than stubborn ones. They will also end up being responsible adults who have a lot of respect and appreciation for their parents as Taureans already have strong ties with their families from the second they are born. Children born under this star sign are affectionate and cuddly even as babies, so all it takes for them to grow up and become considerably achieving adults is to be loved and respected in their own homes.

Taurus Children at School

When it comes to education, Taurus children respond particularly well to sensory learning. They are children with really heightened sensory skills and can learn a lot by using every single one of their five senses. Kids belonging to this zodiac sign are both logical and methodical learners. It can drive their parents and teachers crazy at times when they do not respond well to homework or practical work assigned to them. Yet, adults can easily notice how they still achieve great results with tests, for example. That is because these children take in the information, fully understand it, and analyze it in their tiny little brains, then move on with their lives. They might not all be geniuses or book worms - maybe some are - but they follow a systematic approach in learning that works slowly and steadily until they eventually win the race.

Subjects like math and physics can be where these Taureans shine the greatest. Alternatively, they can do great in sports and art classes and have a great musical ear. They might not be as great when it comes to theoretical subjects and things like learning languages or history and such. Because they are logical and like to count their every move, they work much better with the sciences and can achieve excellent results in such subjects.

Taurus Boy Traits

A male Taurus is an individual with a mind of his own. As children, Taurus boys won't be pushed around under any circumstances. They will do things in their own way and on their own time, or the parents must suffer through hell on earth. Parents can overcome this issue with their boys by showing them a lot of love and affection. Over time, their attitude will improve, and they will learn to compromise for the sake of their loved ones, but only their loved ones. Taurus boys will never be bullied or stand for the bullying of anyone else either. They are the ultimate definition of an alpha male. Leave them in a room with other kids their age, and they will dominate in a matter of minutes.

Generally, boys love their mothers more than anyone else in the whole world. This bond can be even stronger with a Taurus boy than any other kid born under a different star sign. This results from Taureans wanting a lot of love and compassion because it brings them a lot of joy and satisfaction. They are confident in themselves, and that confidence begins with the love that a mother shows them during their early years. A dad's attention is essential too, but motherly love is what can make a difference in a Taurus boy's upbringing.

With their social circle, whether at school or with their friends or relatives anywhere, Taureans are not one who will stand shy in a corner waiting for someone to include them. They know how to make their way into a group and even lead the room on certain occasions. Attention is not exactly what they seek, though they like to be respected and acknowledged in everything they do.

Taurus Girl Traits

A Taurus girl is born to rule from day one. She is not one to be told what to do. People work on her schedule, not the other way around. Organization is her middle name, even as a child. It is also essential to realize from early on that if a baby Taurus female does not like something, no amount of persistence by the parents will ever change her mind. This can apply to food, toys, and even specific places. She will be very vocal about her feelings and won't shy away from an argument.

The Taurus girls are great listeners. They like being told stories, especially when it was from or about their parents when they were younger. They can also be close to their grandparents. If a Taurus girl is the parent's firstborn, the grandparents will probably spoil her rotten with lots of cuddles and love that a Taurus girl will adore.

These young women can be cute, yet so mature for their age. You cannot deceive them because they will bust you almost instantaneously with their sharp mind. They are tenacious and determined, so no matter what creative skills and tricks the parents come up with to get them to do something different, their attempts are likely to fail. The Taurus girl often finds it somewhat amusing to witness their parents' failed attempts to drive them off their course and simply give up in the end to the girl's wishes, but they are not wild children. They are predictable and enjoy stability and discipline in all arrays of life as they grow up.

Hobbies and Interests

One of the many great things about Taurus children is that they are committed to whatever they put their minds to. As soon as they develop an interest in something or have a specific hobby, they are not likely to back out as other children might. Sometimes, this can make them seem a little obsessive which might not always go well with the parents, but it is essential to realize this trait is healthy. It helps them commit to more necessary things in life as they grow old and never back away from anything they've started.

Taurus children are often interested in activities and hobbies that involve set rules and disciplines to them. Chaotic games and messy activities are not something they'll ever enjoy. They enjoy mind games and puzzles that fire up their logical thinking skills, where they can analyze everything and conduct smart tactics. Board games and card games might also seem exciting for them though it might differ from one child to another.

Among the hobbies they might take on and show a keen interest in from early on are artistic hobbies. They might enjoy painting or playing music. That is something that the parents will need to notice and nourish from the early stages in their little kid's life. If these skills and hobbies are well nourished by parents, the kids can grow up to be brilliant and creative people who produce unmatchable artwork.

Stability and Routine

Change is not something that any Taurean appreciates. As soon as they can express themselves a little, even as toddlers, they will show signs of liking stability and routine rather than surprises and sudden changes. Familiarity is everything for these kids, whether it is with people, places, or even food. Taking them to new places to meet new people can be quite a challenge. Though, this might get easier as they grow a little older and go to daycare or school. As soon as Taureans find themselves comfortable with those around them and develop a sense of familiarity, they become the friendliest kids in the world and can talk and laugh and simply be themselves. Otherwise, they won't be comfortable in any new environment, and it will quickly show in their attitude.

Developing a routine with a Taurus kid is one of the easiest things a parent can do. It is recommended so that both the child and the parent can live in harmony together. This routine should be applied to everything from setting a tight sleeping schedule to planning meals every day and making sure the day goes according to a set plan with almost no room for surprises. This routine can make a parent's life so easy, especially with Taurus toddlers since it will allow them to plan their days according to their babies. They'll also be able to find some time for themselves occasionally in the middle of the busy schedules.

Exploring the Senses

Taurus kids experience everything in life through their senses. They will smell, taste, hear, see, and feel every little thing and every detail around them. As soon as they are born, they will start grabbing things and putting everything they see in their mouths after analyzing it with their eyes and noses. As they become toddlers and manage to support their body weight to crawl, anything within eye level from them will probably go into their mouths.

With taste, these kids love to eat. So, parents are not likely to face any issues with them in that regard, but they might find themselves in love with a small selection of food items and not want to try anything else for a while. Parents need to keep on offering their kids healthy alternatives occasionally, without forcing them, and they will eventually come to try them on their own.

These children might also cling to certain toys or cuddly bears as they explore their senses and look for extra affection. Parents should not deprive their kids of that and instead try to encourage them to develop their senses healthily. They can do this by offering them educational toys that can allow them to utilize all their senses effectively.

Emotional Stability

Taurus children have very grounded personalities. They like things done a certain way and only like a selection of items, so if they are offered alternatives or surprised by sudden changes in plans, they can throw manic tantrums. Taurus kids usually are very calm and emotionally stable just if everything is being done their way, and they are getting enough love and affection. The minute there is a change in their routine, they can quickly turn destructive and aggressive until parents cave and give them what they want.

It is the responsibility of the parents to avoid encouraging this behavior. They can do so by having rational discussions with their kids. It's crucial to explain everything logically and lay down all the facts and consequences. Appropriately punishing the children when they become aggressive might also be necessary. This needs to be done to manage these episodes of anger and teach Taurus children rational self-expression.

Staying Active Outdoors

Among the things that Taureans, as kids, excel at is being active outdoors. They are not lazy children who sit at home all day doing nothing or merely playing video games. These kids are explorers who like to feed their natural curiosity by going outside and learning about the world. They may not turn out to be athletes, but they can still do well at certain sports. Simply going outside and soaking in the sunlight can be everything they need to thrive.

Taureans are earthly beings that enjoy everything this planet offers. Exploring the great outdoors by using all their senses is something that will allow them to develop their positive traits and learn more about the world. These children particularly love being outdoors with their parents as they can form a bond with their family and earth as their primary element. Consider taking your children to the backyard or to the park where they can see you in natural surroundings and maybe even hear some fun music in the background while they play and stay active. This can be great for a developing Taurus child.

Physical Traits

Young Taureans are charmers. They have attractive features and almost always take the family's best genes. Since they love being active and engaging with the world outdoors, they are usually fit and maintain a healthy figure growing up. Even with food, although they can be picky eaters, they typically prefer healthy meal options. Their faces are super friendly and cute, making them easily approachable by other youngsters their age at school or any playground.

Artistic Skills

Creativity and innovation are second to any Taurus. That is why they can become great artists or make a successful career for themselves in that sector. It all starts when they are young, even as early as when they are toddlers. They will be way too interested in music and dancing. They can also be keen on drawing and creating their own little masterpieces. Some might even show an interest in cooking by helping their parents in the kitchen then attempting to prepare their meals. Their parents should encourage all these artistic skills so they can develop into successful artists.

Taurus children are born natural artists and just need the right guidance to flourish. They might not necessarily grow up to be painters or dancers, or even singers. They may find their calling in the creative sector in general. If their skills are nurtured and supported as kids, they will grow to become innovative adults. All it takes is some parental support and guidance in the right direction when they notice they have a keen artistic sense in one form of art or another.

Best Toys for Taurus Children

All children love toys; there is no exception to that fact. The only thing that differs from one child to another is the type of toys they enjoy playing with. With young Taureans, they enjoy toys that tickle their five senses and artistic skills. Little musical instruments might be the best toys for babies and toddlers. They will have so much fun grabbing the musical kit and playing songs all day long. Coloring books and drawing sketches might not be toys, but they are something that an older Taurus child would enjoy.

The Taurus kids might also enjoy toys they can use outdoors to get active. Getting them a bike is a great step for the parents since they'll have a fun time playing outside and staying fit. Parents might also consider letting their little Taurus children play in the garden or the dirt. Get them digging toys and a kid-friendly gardening kit.

The Best Books for Taurus Children

Little Taurus children often surprise their parents with how much they love to read. Even those who are too young to read books themselves enjoy having some quality time with their favorite adults who read bedtime stories for them. Books about exploring nature and fictional characters in the wild can be quite intriguing for Taurus kids, and it will help them with their vocabulary and understand the world around them. These children also love gardening considering their element is Earth. Books about gardening and trees will be perfect to teach them a thing or two about nature. This is bound to keep them keen and eager to take on tasks like gardening and caring for plants on their own.

Best Activities for Taurus Children

Parents often want their kids to commit to any beneficial activity when they are young to develop their skills early on and nourish them as they mature. Some parents take their kids to different educational classes, like learning new languages or new skills. Others enroll their children into sports teams to see if they have a knack for sports and maybe a future of being an athlete. Children born under this earthly star sign are big fans of artistic and outdoor activities. So, when parents are choosing a suitable activity for their Taurus boys or girls, they should remember that.

Creative classes, whether it is drawing, singing, dancing, or music, are an excellent option for these kids. These courses won't require them to be too active, yet they will get enough activity to thrive as they grow up. It is a way for them to unleash their inner artists and begin a successful creative journey in that sector.

Another activity that works perfectly for these kids is any outdoor activity that takes them into the wilderness. Things like hiking, camping, fishing, and gardening can be of real interest to the Taurus children from a very young age and can help shape them as they grow up.

Parenting Tips

Raising a child is no easy task. It is full of emotional and physical challenges for both parents, and it is something anyone expecting a child should remember before their babies are even born. For raising a child born under the Taurus zodiac sign, particular challenges might be more manageable than others. As your child grows older, your parenting skills need to change and develop to keep up with their needs. Every minute your little Taurus child grows up, you will need to treat them differently according to his or her developing maturity.

Early Years

Baby Taureans need a lot of love and affection. As they grow older over the years, they will need that outpouring of love and affection, but as infants, they need it a lot more than any other time in their lives. If parents cuddle their newborns and shower them with love and kisses, they are likely to stay calm and even smile and laugh for them all the time. As soon as your babies become toddlers, encourage them to develop their hobbies and interests, and get them to stay active as much as possible. This will allow them to use all their senses and grow up to become more creative and aware.

Teenage Years

Being a teenager is hard on both parents and kids, and that is always the case. When you have a Taurus child verging on their teenage years, they are likely to show a different side of their personality as they try to learn more about themselves. It is a period where they want to be loved and supported by their parents and try to seek some independence from them to do things their way. Stubbornness might be the highlight of this period with Taurus teenagers, and it is the parents' job to manage this behavior with them by having logical discussions and laying down all the facts.

Youth Years

As your child gets to the end of their teenage years and becomes an adult or a young adult, they will leave from under your wing slowly, which is not something that many parents find easy to accept. But parents must realize that their children will always love them and appreciate them even if they are not living under the same roof and following the same rules. The quicker they accept that the better parents they can be for them in their journey of growing older and experiencing the world as tenacious bulls.

Being blessed with a Taurus child is an exciting and adventurous experience. If you have been a Taurus baby yourself, you can realize how the journey of growing up can be a rollercoaster of emotions and challenges. Taureans are easy to raise if they are well understood and supported by their parents. They are just like any other kid needing lots of love and affection to thrive in the world and become successful adults with stability in their lives.

Chapter 5: Taurus in Love

Relationships are what make life a wonderful journey. Finding someone you love that loves you back can be one of the best things about embarking on a new relationship. If you fall for a Taurus, then you should count yourself lucky. These celestial bulls are all about good taste, so that a Taurus is falling for you too says a lot. Those born under this earthy zodiac sign can be great partners. They are loving, loyal, and kind to their loved ones. It is doubtful for a Taurus to be described as a heartbreaker. Whether you are a Taurus yourself or think you are falling for one, here is everything you should know about Taureans in love.

What they Look for in a Relationship

Taureans love being in love. Affection means a lot to them, and they will do anything to get it and shower their lover with it. When Taureans dive into a relationship, they are in it for the long run. Flings and one-night stands do not interest these celestial characters as they are all about stability and commitment. They will not pressure their partner into committing too quickly or suffocate them with how much they want a long-term relationship. Although, they will clarify it from the first minute of that relationship they are after a stable commitment built to last.

While you are together, a Taurus won't ever stop fighting for you. It is a known fact that Taureans are stubborn, but if you are dating one, think of that stubbornness as passion. They will do anything for their loved ones and continuously work on improving their relationship with their partner. It is fair to say they come first in the zodiac calendar competition of the best lovers.

Why they are Great Lovers

The perfect lover criteria often differ from one person to another. But some fundamentals make a great partner – which everyone can attest to. These fundamentals are what make the relationship so strong and stable for those looking for long-term commitments. Being romantically involved with a Taurus should make you expect certain things you would not usually get with anyone born under a different star sign. Here are characteristics you should expect:

Loyalty

Trust is the basis of any healthy relationship. Those who want stability and peace of mind in their lives always seek loyal and committed partners they can count on and trust with their hearts. That is something that can be easily found in a Taurus. They are intensely loyal and devoted to the person they are with, against all odds. They do not need a "for better or worse" vow considering that is just how they operate anyway. As soon as they find someone who makes them happy, they are theirs for the long haul and will notice no one else under any circumstance.

Romantic

First impressions of a Taurus may not always reveal just how sensitive and romantic they are but being in a relationship with one is often like living in a fairytale. Taurus individuals are all about affection and showering their partners with love, and they are never afraid to show it at every chance they get. They are touchy-feely and love to cuddle with their other halves to express how much they care about them. They also appreciate the nice things in life. So, expect a Taurus to spend a lot of money on their partners, showering them with fancy gifts and trips every now and then just to spoil them and treat them right. The only thing a Taurus expects in return is mutual love and respect and showing appreciation for all their efforts.

Depth of Emotion

Talking about emotions and being vulnerable around others is not something that many people can do. For dating someone, they must show you this side of them and be open with you so you can get to know them fully. Taureans have no problem opening up to their loved ones and having deep conversations about their emotions or becoming vulnerable around them. They won't expose their feelings that deeply unless it is with someone they fully trust and love. So once a Taurus opens up to you, know just how special you are to them. These conversations are what can make a relationship with a Taurus stronger, and you'll both be ready to face everything that life throws in your way.

Ambitious

Being in a long-term relationship with someone means having to think about the future at one point or another. It is not just what the future has in store for the relationship itself, but what it will be like for the individuals in this partnership in terms of their careers and personal lives. Planning is something of second nature to a Taurus. They are extremely ambitious and always look forward to becoming better and more successful at anything they set their minds to, whether it's a career or a personal endeavor. Surprises are not something they like, so they will have a set plan for everything they would like to achieve and accomplish in their life. If they have someone they care about, they will include them in that plan for sure.

Passionate

Taureans are stubborn; that is an undeniable fact. Still, if you are in a relationship with one, this stubbornness is more likely to turn into a passion. Those born under this zodiac sign fight for everything they believe in at all costs. So, if they believe you are the one for them, they will fight for you tooth and nail, remaining dedicated to you against all odds. It will not matter what the world thinks about your relationship or what anyone ever says to bring him or her down. Once they have their heart and mind set on someone they believe is partner material, they will show their passion for them and do anything it takes to keep them around.

Dedicated

A Taurus is known to be a hard worker, but hard work does not just stop at the office or at them being a little workaholic. They carry that trait in everything aspect of their lives. Dedication to their loved ones comes naturally to a Taurus, so their partners should never have to worry about them not putting enough effort into the relationship or giving it their all. These Taurus individuals do not go through anything unless they are not willing to put their hearts and souls into it and tirelessly give it everything they have. That includes their romantic relationships where they'll be obsessed with their other half, in a healthy manner, and will likely do anything for them.

Mysterious

The initial period in any relationship is always full of mystery and electricity. The couple wants to learn all about each other and impress each other with their character and personality. Taureans can be a little mysterious at first and not show all their cards at once. They will still try to impress whoever they have their eyes on, but they will not open up too soon. Once they do confide in their partner and share things about their past and what they are like, one can quickly see they have a lot more than what meets the eye. It is one of Taureans' most attractive things since they only allow certain people to knock down their walls and get a glimpse into their souls.

Turn-Ons and Turn-Offs

Loving a Taurus is not a complicated task. They are simple beings that only need some love and appreciation to thrive in any relationship. The biggest turn on for a Taurus is the ability to understand them so well and being sensual around them. Planning simple dates not too extravagant or too cheap can be the best thing a partner does for their Taurus lover. Taureans are very conscious about their finances, so they do not need someone to spend crazy amounts of money on them to make them happy. Instead, they would rather spend long hours with their lovers talking about important things and spending quality time together in the mornings and evenings.

When it comes to a Taurean's turn-offs, they are not ones who appreciate feeling like they are "plan B." They do not expect their lovers to prioritize them a hundred percent of the time either, but it is always nicer when they are right up there on their second half's priority list. Nothing can get on a Taurean's nerves more than canceling plans at the last minute. These earthy characters are all about planning and hate surprises to their very core. So, if they plan and trust they are doing something with their partners and they cancel it suddenly, it can start massive arguments. Similarly, Taureans love it when their lovers put effort into the relationship. So, if at any point they get the feeling that their partner is not putting in any thought as to how they woo their second half and instead settle for just anything, a Taurus will close off from the relationship and lose interest quickly.

Best Matches

Finding your perfect match can be challenging. Everyone wants to be loved and understood so they can thrive in a healthy relationship. That is why people often go on tons of dates before they can finally say they have found "the one." But analyzing your star sign compared to other star signs can be just the thing you need to find your other half. Every star sign has some compatibility with other star signs; it is just about finding that perfect celestial match made in heaven. Since a Taurus's main element is Earth, they get along well with fellow earthy signs. Here are some of the best matches for a Taurus and how their relationship will be like.

Virgo

Virgos and Taureans can be the most peaceful couple you ever get to meet. They both hate drama and are all about being straightforward with one another. This pair of earthy beings are as sophisticated as they come. They are logical thinkers who weigh all the facts and have rational discussions concerning their relationship. People will often describe this couple as a lovely duo. They like minding their own business but are super friendly to others, and it shows in the way they treat everyone around them. They are extremely traditional, and if they live together, their spirits will reflect in their home through a display of creativity and warmth. Occasionally, the couple can be a little judgmental, but it won't be too aggressive or offensive to anyone. Taurus and Virgo are open-minded and intellectual people, which is likely because Venus rules them both.

Pisces

These two-star signs are a sensual match ruled by the planets, Venus and Neptune. Taureans and Pisces getting together can only mean one thing, and that is living a luxurious and comfy life. This couple fancies gourmet meals and has a knack for expensive wines and sophisticated events. Taureans do not always flaunt their love for lavishness, but with a little encouragement from their Pisces partners, they can go all out. Those born under the Pisces star sign are imaginative and in touch with their emotions. This makes them perfect for Taureans who love talking about in-depth topics and delving into their emotions with their trusted partner. This couple is amazingly dynamic and in control of their relationship in a way that does not allow emotional build-up to ever hinder their love.

Capricorn

Taureans are known for being stubborn occasionally. Capricorns are perfect for them in that regard as they can easily match their persistence and reach a compromising balance with them every time. This duo goes well together, especially with their love and passion for work. They can both be workaholics, but their ambition and determination to succeed in their relative careers is what might bring them together in the first place. Financial stability is the number one priority for this duo, so you are not likely to find them arguing over money as they are both quite sensible with their expenditure. Although both star signs love organization and plan for every little detail, Capricorns can have a bit more discipline than Taureans. It would not cause arguments, but Capricorns tend to push their fellow Taurus partner to do more and stay motivated than they would outside the relationship.

Taurus

Occasionally, the stars will align for a bull and bull match to happen, the perfect definition of a power couple. This pair is all about being slow and steady. They are in the relationship for the long run and are committed to one another. They are a power couple due to their love for love. They appreciate the beauty of one another and can be affectionate behind closed doors. Ruled by Venus, they usually live in a house more of an art gallery than a home. As Taureans have high artistic senses and appreciate the beauty in everything, they like displaying their creativity if they live under the same roof. The home of a Taurus couple is usually the heart of family gatherings. This pair loves their blood ties and looks forward to bringing everyone together on all occasions. They can host lavish parties and reunions always warm and inclusive. The power pair are also likely to be great parents, as they can set an example in love and discipline that any kid would be lucky to have.

Worst Matches

Just as there are star signs that are always compatible together, there are ones that just don't. Some of these matches might be nice and dreamy initially but can become a failed relationship too soon. There are some exceptions to these rules if one person, usually not a Taurus, will compromise to make the relationship work. Yet, these exceptions are so rare, and when found, the relationship might not be as happy or healthy as one would want. If you ever find yourself involved with someone from an opposite star sign, you will need to give yourself some time to think about what you might be getting yourself into and whether or not this relationship is doomed from the start.

Gemini

Stability is everything for someone born under the Taurus zodiac sign. They are very traditional beings that are very grounded and love having everything done so it fits with their chill lifestyle. Geminis are the opposite of that; they are outgoing individuals who are hot and cold and all about new adventures. Pairing those two together can be a disaster in the making. At first, they may think that they are balancing each other out, but eventually, clashes are bound to happen, and it can break the relationship completely. Free-spirited Geminis and traditional Taureans are rare to have many things in common, if anything at all, and that is not a good foundation to start a healthy relationship with.

Leo

The chemistry between those two celestial star signs can be great, but that chemistry can lead to a nuclear explosion in the end. Stubbornness is something they share, and compromise is not something that any of them is ever willing to do. Lions love being in charge but so do bulls. When placed together in one pair, it can end in one of two ways, either a complete disaster where arguing is the only thing these two ever do or taking over the world together as one fierce, dynamic duo. The success of a lion and a bull in a romantic relationship is a rare event, but it is possible. But usually these two signs do not see eye to eye as they are always in a power play that rarely ends well.

Libra

Taureans and Libras are both ruled by the planet Venus, which is famously known for its great passion and sensuality. However, with these two signs, the cardinal elements are just not suitable for each other, with one being Earth and the other being air. This makes a relationship between those two an uncomfortable and often an unsuccessful one. Earthly signs always look for stability and traditions, whereas those following the cardinal element of air are always buzzing for change and adventure. It can be frustrating when these two come together as they want to feel loved and share their love of nature, but it often comes across in the wrong way, leading to their inevitable separation.

Scorpio

A Scorpio and a Taurus's traits can be seen as opposites; these two just won't get along on much of anything. It is not only in romantic relationships, it's even in social relationships, that they go neck to neck. The two-star signs often have a love-hate relationship because of their differences, but that is often a deal-breaker for them for getting romantic. Each is always trying to mark their territory and prove that they are in control, which never works in a healthy coupling.

Loving a Taurus Woman

Falling for a Taurus woman can be the best feeling in the world. These women are affectionate and caring and will shower their partner with unconditional love. It is not the suffocating love that people often escape from, but it's the kind that humans need to feel special and wanted. If you are lucky enough to love a Taurus woman, then you should always make her feel like the queen she is. Never try to change her or tell her she is not enough; she does not like feeling she must compete for your love. Also, public displays of affection will not always feel right for her. Though, remember that compliments are always nice to hear anywhere, especially if her loved one praises her in front of her close family and friends, whom she holds dearly in her heart.

Loving a Taurus Man

The way to a Taurus man's heart is through emotional support and appreciation. These men can seem a little standoffish when you first meet them, but when they fall for you, all their walls will be broken down. They expect their partners to take them and make them feel understood and loved through all odds. Small gestures will go a long way in your relationship with a Taurus guy. Things like asking about their day or giving them little compliments every now and then can make all the difference in the world. These men thrive on routine and stability, so surprising them is not a good idea. Instead, try to plan things together and see what they love to do on their time off so you can work on your relationship more often and bond in a healthy manner.

Attracting a Taurus

Taureans are all about long-term commitment. If you are looking to settle down and maybe even get married at some point, then he or she can be your perfect match. Attracting them can be done by showing them you are looking for the same things they are. Being a grounded person on good terms with their family and likes expressing their feelings to others appropriately and healthily can get you on top of a Taurean's list. They are suckers for family-oriented individuals passionate about the important things in life. These celestial beings also love being involved with someone who cares about their career and has a lot of ambition that allows them to succeed in life.

Signs a Taurus is Interested

A Taurus is not too obvious for showing how they feel. They take their time and try to be subtle at first just to see how the other person responds. Taureans like giving subtle hints to test the waters, and once they feel like the person on the other end are interested too, they will go all in. Some signs they will give are things like checking up on the person they are interested in more often. They'll send texts and messages and show a lot of interest in their lives and how their days are going so they can let the person know they care about them.

A Taurus often shows they are into someone by asking him or her for advice occasionally. Taureans are very stubborn and mostly do whatever they want and like to do. So, if they genuinely ask for advice from someone they are interested in, it is a clear sign they are falling hopelessly in love.

Perfect Date Ideas

Dating a Taurus can be a magical time. They are all about showing love and affection to their other half, and for planning a date, they expect a whole lot of romance to be involved. They are also active people who like going out in nature and spending some quality time with their partners. That is why planning a date with your Taurus lover is simple if you know them. Here are some date ideas guaranteed to tickle a Taurean's fancy.

Hiking

Going out in the secluded nature trails with their favorite person can be the perfect date for a Taurus. It can be packed with delicious snacks and some candles or roses to make it even more romantic. Essentially, this kind of date just ticks all the boxes. It gets the Taurus to go out and get active and use all their senses and allows them to feel free while being showered with love from their partner.

Movie Night

Romance is a Taurus's middle name. They are also big fans of traditions and love being at home where they can be themselves. Bringing all those elements together in a magical movie night with a nice dinner can be the best thing you do for your favorite Taurus. It is romantic and cozy and is all about showering each other with love and attention away from the rest of the world.

Couples Massage

There is nothing more relaxing and enjoyable than getting your sore muscles massaged at a spa, especially with your loved one. This date idea allows a Taurus and their partner to get in touch with all their senses and relax together in a calm setup that fits their relationship's theme. It is the perfect getaway to let loose together and come out feeling refreshed and more connected to your partner.

Falling for a Taurus can be an exciting experience. It is also likely to last for a long time, a lifetime if the stars are aligned for you. When dating a Taurus, it is vital that you let them be themselves without judging or asking them to change. They will do anything for their loved ones, but not if they feel insecure. Remember always to express your love for your Taurus partner through compliments and showing care for them through all the odds because that will give them all the reassurance they need that they are loved and wanted.

Chapter 6: Taurus at Work

After covering Taurus's personal life in the previous chapters, let's peek into the professional side of this zodiac sign. In this chapter, we will discuss a Taurean's career and workplace characteristics.

In general, a Taurus is a hard-working, reliable, and determined employee or boss in the work field. However, certain weaknesses could massively ruin their chances of gaining success. Let's take a detailed look at how the Taurus is like in the work field and what can stop them from achieving success.

Best Career Choices for the Taurus

A Taurus is ambitious, dependable, and hard-working, which makes them great workers and leaders on the professional front. Based on their traits, a Taurus should focus on these career paths.

1. Chef or Restaurant Manager

Taureans love and appreciate food. They like to try new recipes and are often curious about different cuisines. Among other zodiac signs, Taurus individuals are the emerging food aficionados. And so, they can make great chefs, as they love to cook and feed others. Besides preparing delectable dishes, they will also ensure that the presentation of each dish is optimized. If they don't want to cook but still manage projects around food (due to their knowledge and liking for food), they can also make talented restaurant managers. Taureans have impeccable organization and planning skills. They can easily manage and instruct restaurant workers, waiters, cleaners, and other staff.

Candace Nelson and Brad Leone are two famous Taurus chefs.

2. Interior Designer

Since Taurus holds an apprehension for art and culture, they make amazing designers. Interior design is an excellent choice for this zodiac sign due to their impressive organizational skills and ability to transform a space. They also have a knack for talking to homeowners and convincing them to follow a particular home transformation plan. While individuals with Cancer and Libra as zodiac signs are also equally talented at this job, the Taurus can pave their path in this discipline due to their desire for perfection. Besides interior designers, Taureans can also work as fashion and graphic designers. Since they are keen on knowing and learning about aesthetics, this career option is an excellent fit for a Taurus.

Donatella Versace and Tan France are two famous Taurus fashion designers who are well known for their knowledge of aesthetic and styling skills.

3. Banker or Financial Advisor

Also known as a manager of money, a person with this zodiac sign can look into money handling and organization as a plausible career option. Due to their meticulous and pragmatic attitude, Taureans can also become competent bankers or financial advisors. Since they are wise and resilient, they have been deemed an asset within this discipline. Besides bankers and financial advisors, they can also look into financial administration and accountancy as a career option in this field. Another reason this option is great for the Taurus is that they are skilled in the calculation and tremendously reliable for accuracy.

4. Botanist or Agriculturist

This sign loves nature and wants to be around flora and fauna. If you are a Taurus and are partial to spending most of your time outdoors and around nature, this career option is the most suitable. Besides their passion for nature, their meticulous skills and knack for details will make them talented botanists and researchers in this field. This discipline requires a person to follow a pattern and take a methodical approach, which is a perfect career option for a Taurus. Other suitable sub-disciplines include farming, landscaping, and gardening.

5. Politician or Leader

Taureans are known to be stubborn and do not budge until they convince the other person. At times, this can lead to arguments. But if a Taurus uses this trait for their benefit, they can become a successful politician. Also, their organization and attention to detail will help them make better decision-makers. They are independent, determined, and quick on their feet. As a Taurus, if you pursue a goal, you will go to any extent to achieve it. This is a much-needed trait in most politicians. If becoming a politician is not their cup of tea, they also make competent leaders, such as the CEO of a company or an entrepreneur.

Some famous Taurus politicians include Pope John Paul II and Queen Elizabeth II.

6. Singer, Composer, or Musician

Taureans are artistic and have a great sense of style, music, food, and other cultural interests. Even though they are pragmatic by nature, their artistic sense is exemplary, which is also surprising. With music, they are extremely gifted. If you need new song suggestions, you can always turn to a Taurus. This quality can also be turned into a successful career as a musician or singer. And they can work for endless hours with the same scrutiny and attention to detail, which is required in a music career. You will find them working until they have achieved perfection.

James Brown, Billy Joel, and Sam Smith are some famous Taurus musicians and singers.

7. Manager or Executive

As mentioned, Taureans are blessed with management skills and can be extremely resourceful. This makes roles like management and executive direction fit for this zodiac sign. Also, since they are not shy, they like to take the plunge and lead others within this discipline. A manager or an executive must stay on top of their game and lead their team, which is another reason it makes a perfect job description. Also, since these two positions offer a higher chance of getting a bonus or a promotion, the Taurus usually prefers it.

8. Makeup Artist or Beauty Blogger

A Taurus has an impeccable aesthetic taste and a knack for beauty. They focus not only on their looks, but they also have a distinct perception of beauty around them. When paired with their eye for detail, they can make talented makeup artists or beauty bloggers. This zodiac sign's ruling planet is Venus, which explains their tenacity of becoming a beauty blogger. Anything related to beauty is a great career choice for a Taurus, but know that succeeding in this discipline will take some time. Even though it will be difficult initially, you will enjoy every bit of this journey, which will make it easier for you to succeed. This is also partly due to your tenacious nature.

9. Vet or Pet Sitter

Your love for animals can be converted into a career option. Two such options include being a veterinarian or a pet sitter. While the former requires you to have enough patience to study and graduate, the latter does not require formal education. Both these options let you be near pets most of the time, which is something a Taurus will love. Also, a Taurus is reliable, which makes them great pet sitters. As an individual with this zodiac sign, you can also consider other similar jobs, like pet grooming, dog boarding, or pet taxi. Since you are also blessed with management and organizational skills, you can make relevant appointments and start your own pet company. Consider other options like dog training classes and grooming equipment stores as well.

Worst Career Choices for the Taurus

1. Doctor, Nurse, or Medical Practitioner

Any sub-category within the medical discipline requires time and patience and is not a strong suit for Taurus. Individuals with this zodiac sign work hard to achieve their goals; however, they are not well known for practicing patience. First, it takes years to graduate as a doctor or medical practitioner, which is difficult for this zodiac sign. Second, they want to achieve their goals within a lesser time, which may lead to rushing mistakes. Any kind of error is unavoidable in the medical field.

2. Human Resources

A job role as an HR sounds boring and mundane, which a Taurus will hate. Since people with this zodiac sign usually look forward to new and challenging tasks, this job may be too modest for them. An HR's responsibility is to narrow down the gap between the company and employees, which needs time and patience. While the Taurus can easily manage the organizational skills and even excel at it, they might just not have the patience to deal with employees' complaints. Let's not forget about a Taurus' stubbornness that could potentially get in the way of their job role and cause trouble in the company.

3. Teacher or Professor

Again, this role is difficult for the Taurus to portray, as it needs them to be more tolerant and accepting of others. Since kids don't easily listen to elders, it can be difficult for them to manage such scenarios. Also, if a kid and a Taurus come face to face, their stubborn natures can cause a never-ending debate. No one is ready to yield, which can cause trouble for the Taurus as a teacher.

These best and worst career options for this zodiac sign should be considered when picking a field. Consider your skills and strengths at a personal level and make a wise choice.

Where Does the Taurus Fit in an Office Setting?

Various scenarios in an office setting involve employees being near the water cooler and gossiping about other employees, planning social events, and managing informal gathering, or putting on headphones and are engrossed in their work. Where do you find a Taurus in such workplace scenarios?

The Taurus loves their share of gossip and will want to discuss it with their close friends. If one of their coworkers is also their best friend, you are likely to see them in the office cafeteria or near the water cooler, where they occasionally meet to pass along fresh news. Also, since they are social, they always look forward to parties and informal gatherings. If you need a party planner in an office setting, hire a Taurus. Their impeccable organizational and management skills make them competent event planners. It is difficult to find a Taurus engrossed in only work.

Since they can be lazy, dependent, and often too distracted, they are less likely to be seated at their desks, completing their work. They either hover around the workplace, looking for others to finish the task or are distracted by their phone or other unimportant matters.

A Taurus boss is rarely seen in the office, which gives other Taurus employees the freedom to roam around and complete tasks at his or her own pace. Also, since the boss is usually unaware of the day-to-day tasks and accomplishments, it is easier for a Taurus to take credit.

Obstacles at Work

A Taurus at the office or a work setting can be surprising. While they have many strengths, their weaknesses can often overpower their personality. This affects not only their work and productivity but also their mental health. To resolve these weaknesses, first learn how to detect them.

If you are a Taurus or are working around one, you may notice one or more of these obstacles or weaknesses in their work and performance.

Taurus as a Coworker or Employee

1. They May be "Bonus Oriented"

Due to their materialistic nature and need to live a luxurious life, most individuals with this zodiac sign constantly seek a bonus or a promotion. For this, they often overwork and try to achieve their goals quickly. While it is beneficial for the company, it might affect the quality of work. If they fail to achieve their bonus, they might get extraordinarily disappointed or disheartened, dampening their productivity and will to work.

2. They Can be Too Lazy

A Taurean's lazy nature can pose a threat in their path towards success. Although most Taurus employees are ambitious, they often get lazy during group projects or when it is a collective responsibility. They may rely on their coworkers to get the job done, which can delay the deadline. Even if they agree to contribute, their lazy nature can disturb their working pattern, which will cause unsatisfactory results. If a Taurus puts 100% effort into his or her work (which many achieve), he or she will probably be the best employee in a workplace setting. However, their laziness often keeps them from being one.

3. They Can Easily Get into Fights

Due to their stubborn nature, a Taurus can easily pick up a fight with their coworker. Debates and arguments are frequent with a Taurus as a teammate. They not only argue with their coworker but can also get in occasional tiffs with their boss. It is difficult to win an argument with a Taurus, even if you are right. While it hardly matters in an informal setting, this attitude can majorly affect a company's performance and goals.

4. They Can be Too Social

While it doesn't harm their personal life, a social employee might be seen chatting and making plans during office hours. They are often distracted during work due to their need to be social. If one of their coworkers is also one of their closest friends, they are often seen socializing, which can affect their quality of work.

5. They are Dependent and Take Undeserving Credit

A Taurus has the potential to develop innovative ideas; however, they are occasionally not bothered to do it and let their coworkers take charge. Besides, if their coworkers complete the project on time and accomplish the goal, the Taurus employee takes the credit.

Taurus as a Boss or Group Leader

1. They May Want to Achieve Too Many Things at Once

As a Taurus boss, your main goal will often involve completing a project or wrapping up a deal as quickly as possible. Taureans are very ambitious go-getters and will fight their way to achieve success. While this is beneficial for the company, it may affect your employees' mental health. Not everyone can work as quickly as a Taurus, and they should understand that your employees have their own pace and can get only a certain number of things done within a designated period. If you're a Taurus boss, try to take things slowly and take one step at a time. Follow a plan to get closer to your goal. Even if it takes time, you are bound to succeed.

2. They Can be Bossy and Insensitive

If your Taurus boss doesn't get what he wants, he may become too bossy and even lose their temper occasionally. When it comes to working, they disregard their employees' and co-founder's feelings and won't think twice before uttering harsh words. While it is casual for them, certain words and remarks could hurt their employee's sentiments, which might even affect their performance. In extreme cases, a Taurus boss can even make personal remarks, which is unacceptable. Employees under all circumstances should abide by their rules and regulations, which are written in stone. Failure to do so could trigger the Taurus boss, resulting in a hard time for the employees. Even if a Taurus rarely gets angry, their casual attitude towards treating other people, especially when the latter are wrong, can come across as mean and rude.

3. They Refrain from Accepting Their Mistakes

Even if they are unclear about their expectations, they are not ready to accept their mistakes initially. The need for the right takes a toll on their employees. A Taurus boss usually briefs their employees in a way they deem "perfect" and "detailed." While it is typically the case, they can sometimes be too vague due to impatience. In this case, the results are unsatisfactory and not up to their expectations. Conversely, a Taurus boss can sometimes blame their employees instead of accepting their mistake.

4. They are Unable to Take Risks

While this can lead to favorable outcomes sometimes, a leader should possess the courage to take risks to lead their company to success. The Taurus boss prefers to play it safe, resulting in losing potentially successful leads and deals. Individuals with this zodiac sign cannot face the fear of uncertainty. Taking risks is all about being aware and affecting, which is not a strong suit for Taurus. While being a risk-taker is rare, a leader or a boss should possess this skill to achieve success.

Once you determine the traits of a Taurus in a work setting, you can then help them resolve these issues so they can lead a successful work life.

Tips for a Fulfilling Work Life

Since a Taurus can be too lazy and stubborn they are likely to face failure in aspects of their career if they don't turn things around. As a Taurus, work on your weaknesses and polish your strengths for personal development and get closer to your goals. Since you already know your weaknesses, it is time to navigate them to gain a fruitful professional life.

Here are some work tips for individuals with this zodiac sign:

1. Take Charge of a Project

While a Taurus can be too lazy to contribute to a project as a coworker, they are the complete opposite as a team leader, as mentioned in the previous chapters. If you want to improve your lazy nature and contribute more to the workforce, take charge of a project. Be a leader and put your organizational skills to proper use. A Taurus team leader is an excellent addition to the company and will become reliable and push their fellow teammates to do their best. This way, a Taurus will learn to pull their weight and drive the company towards success. At the same time, they should initiate new ideas and projects with a detailed plan likely to gain approval.

Taureans make promising leaders, which is why you should work as one. If your boss doesn't recognize your talent and is skeptical about appointing you as the leader, you must prove yourself first. Throw your lazy veil away and work to prove yourself. Come up with innovative ideas and a detailed plan to increase your chances of being appointed as the group leader.

2. Take More Risks

While it is easier said than done, taking risks is imperative in a workplace setting, especially if you are the company's boss or CEO. Since the Taurus lacks the courage to take risks, it is difficult for them to take the leap. To let go of this fear and build courage, try to acknowledge your fear. Being vulnerable and knowing of this feeling can help you build the courage to take risks. If you know the dangers and fear involved in a particular risk, you become more prepared to overcome them. What is the worst that can happen? What could go wrong? To what extent will it harm the company or employees? Questions such as these will also help you overcome the fear of taking risks.

Taking risks will help your company and make you more confident and resilient as a person. It is necessary to develop your personality too. You'd be surprised to know your potential. Last, build more skills and develop your skills to gain the confidence to overcome risky situations. You must be patient, as being a risk-taker is not easy.

3. Learn to Compromise

There is a fine line between being levelheaded and being stubborn. While the former usually relates to being wise and making the right decisions, the latter often leads to a downfall as it relates to the need for being right (even if the person is wrong). As you already know, the Taurus is probably the most stubborn of all zodiac signs. A Taurus should learn to compromise and let things go. Failing to do so can affect their personal and professional life. They may even lose touch with valuable acquaintances and job prospects. If you cannot put your foot down, it is necessary to turn this situation around.

To do this, learn to listen to others. Do not speak or interrupt others before they have finished. Even if you disagree with someone, let him or her speak before you put your viewpoint across. Before you assert domination and mark all prospects as "no", take a minute to evaluate the situation and talk only when you fully agree. At times, spontaneous reactions and quick decisions can lead to misunderstandings and even arguments. So, listen carefully before you speak. Also, know that you are not always right. Remember this when talking to someone. More important, remember that not everyone has to agree with your opinion. Let go of this expectation and learn to compromise.

4. Improve Your Communication Skills

While the Taurus doesn't face an issue to communicate with others, their stubborn nature can cause a rude and mean tone, even if they don't mean it. Improving your communication skills will help you in the professional field to impress your boss. It is a necessity for most zodiac signs.

Besides speaking, effective communication skills also involve proper listening. Let the person finish their lines and focus on the critical parts. Try to maintain eye contact. This shows you are listening to the other person and are acknowledging their opinion. It will also help you focus on the crucial parts of a conversation, which will ultimately help you make acceptable comments. When your time to respond, be humble, and help others realize that you have been listening to the entire time. Whether it's an employee you are talking to or conversing with a delegate on an important business lunch, focus on the way you speak and listen to achieve the best outcome.

5. Overcome Procrastination by Minimizing Distractions

Due to their laziness and need to procrastinate, a Taurus may witness delayed success. Even though they can achieve success through their talent and organizational skills, their laziness can be a significant obstacle. To overcome this, minimize distractions and incorporate anti-procrastination strategies. Since procrastination is deeply ingrained in one's behavioral pattern, it's challenging to turn it around in less time. However, one must try to succeed and achieve their goals.

The first step towards overcoming procrastination is to realize your problem. Once you do, stop beating yourself up and promise yourself to turn the situation around. Second, minimize distractions such as mobile phones, electronics, and food. Since you are lazy to work, you often find distractions that fuel your boredom. To avoid this, keep your cell phone and electronics locked in a drawer and keep food away. Besides this, try other anti-procrastination strategies such as making a to-do list, rewarding yourself for accomplishing specific tasks, or asking someone to keep track of your progress.

These tips will help a Taurus excel at work and push them to achieve their goals. Implementing these tips will also help you to work on your personality and make a positive change in your personal life.

As you learned, the Taurus at work can either make or break the entity they are working for. While they possess numerous strengths, their weaknesses could lead to a major downfall in their performance and productivity. The best way to combat this situation is to recognize these flaws and improve them. If a Taurus does it, they are bound to succeed.

Chapter 7: The Social Taurus

Most Taureans possess unparalleled social skills and a need to make friends. In this chapter, we will look at how a typical Taurus behaves in a party or an informal setting.

Taurus Friendships

In this section, we will talk about how Taurus makes friends and functions in general. When it comes to making friends and sustaining long-term friendships, a Taurus gives 100%. They hardly make friends, but once they do, they are in it for a long haul. Even though they consider "friends forever" to be a cliché, they abide by it. It is challenging to attract a Taurus and be their friend, but the bond is fruitful once you do it. The Bull is not only loyal but also possesses a great sense of humor.

If you are in pain or feeling down, call a Taurean friend to get a dose of laughter because they are witty and know how to make people laugh. Also, they remember important dates, events, birthdays, and anniversaries of people close to them. With a Taurus as your best friend, you can expect a grand celebration on your birthday. They will never let you modestly celebrate any important dates. Even if you don't like it, you must put up with their grandeur and celebrate your day as they prefer. This shows they take friendships seriously and want their friends to stay happy and content.

It is difficult to be friends with a Taurus as they are too picky with people they allow in their inner circle. And so, you must work at winning their heart and gaining their trust. Still, you will always have to put up with their stubbornness, which is difficult. Also, since a Taurus is often suspicious of others and their intentions, being close or best friends with them is a major challenge. For them, outsiders always seem to have an agenda that can affect their personal and professional lives. You can't blame a Taurus for thinking this way, as they often encounter people who take advantage of their loyalty. This weakens their trust in people, which also explains their pickiness. And they are honest and expect honesty from their friends too.

Taurus Friendship Grid with the Other 11 Zodiacs

In this section, we will examine the friendship compatibility of Taurus with other zodiac signs.

Taurus and Aries

Aries is governed by the symbol of Ram, which makes them impulsive and always seeking adventure. While a Taurus prefers to take things slow and experience one step at a time, an Aries usually takes the leap, which often causes an imbalance between them. Though, since Aries is direct and straightforward, you prefer to hang out with them. They directly tell you what's on their mind, which feeds your impatient soul. There is usually no beef between you two. Also, you don't mind exploring new arenas and going on occasional adventures with your Aries' friend. But Aries prefers to hang out with a Taurus due to the latter's carefree and sensible attitude.

Taurus and Taurus

Surprisingly, a friendship between these two similar signs turns out to be relatively stable. You can rely on each other and always count on your Taurean friend when you are sick or in trouble. As a Taurus, if you are looking for practical assistance and advice, you can always turn to another Taurean. They are always aware and quick on their feet to give you the best practical advice possible. Whether job assistance or a suggestion for a good doctor, they always have an answer. Due to their relaxed nature and earthy humor, they enjoy each other's company and look forward to spending time together. Even if you don't like adventures, you won't mind enduring new experiences such as wine tasting, a visit to the amusement park, or a spa retreat with them. One major downside to this friendship is that both friends can get into an unending argument. Due to their stubbornness, none will back off easily.

Taurus and Gemini

A Gemini is known to be whimsical, which is quite the opposite of a Taurus' apparent traits. They are not as practical as you and may make you question their actions. While they are constantly seeking adventure, a Taurus prefers to follow a routine, which is quite the contrary. A Gemini friend prefers to spend money on the best experiences, whereas a Taurus friend prefers to save every penny earned. As you can see, it can be difficult for these signs to become friends. Even with, a Gemini's sense of humor and a Taurus' practical and methodical approach always balance the two, which sustains the friendship. For the friendship to last long, a Taurus must put up with a Gemini's unwillingness and steady movements, whereas a Gemini has to be patient.

Taurus and Cancer

This pairing is one of the few friendship bonds that can last for years, which is rare with this zodiac sign. Cancer always vents or puts their thoughts and aspirations in front of their Taurus friend. The Taurus doesn't mind listening to their Cancer friend even if they call at midnight. Both signs are there for each other through thick and thin. Their friendship is loyal and everlasting. While a Cancer admires your perception towards life, a Taurus friend appreciates the other's executive abilities, which brings a perfect balance to the friendship. If a Taurus manages to put up with a Cancer's moodiness and a Cancer rarely minds a Taurus' stubbornness, the friendship is bound to last long.

Taurus and Leo

Despite being different personalities, certain commonalities between a Leo and a Taurus bring these signs together. Their appreciation for luxury, materials, and the finer things in life is unparalleled, which often brings them together. Also, both signs are highly creative, which brings up interesting topics of discussion, most of which are related to art, museums, photography, and other cultural implications. Both signs also match in terms of impeccable organizational and management skills, which they find attractive about each other. For the friendship to last long, a Taurus must put up with Leo's ego, and a Leo must ignore a Taurus' calculated steps.

Taurus and Virgo

Both signs love nature and being outdoors, which brings them closer. Friends of this zodiac sign are often seen on an adventure, a picnic, or random evening walks. As a Taurus, if you are looking for practical assistance and problem-solving skills, you can always turn to a Virgo. But if a Virgo needs financial advice and management, they can ask their Taurus friend for help. A Taurus may find a Virgo friend annoying because they act as neat freaks. But they tend to ignore these tidbits because a Virgo friend also ignores a Taurus' stubbornness.

Taurus and Libra

Since both signs share the ruling planet Venus, they hold an inordinate desire for beauty and art. Within this discipline, your tastes may marginally vary. For instance, a Libra may prefer exquisite or contemporary artists, whereas a Taurus will stick to antique or classical art and expression forms. While a Libra is more social and is often seen in a bigger group of friends, you prefer to stick to one or two of your closest pals. Even though a Taurus possesses the ability to be social, they prefer to stick to their closest friends. One significant difference between these two signs is that a Taurus is organized, whereas a Libra is all over the place, often without an organized plan. Also, a Libra friend has the tendency to change their mind quickly, which leaves the Taurus friend confused. Since a Taurus prefers to follow a plan, they may find this trait to be annoying. For the friendship to last long, a Taurus must put up with a Libra's spontaneity, and a Libra must let go of a Taurus' attention to detail.

Taurus and Scorpio

Even though a Taurus and a Scorpio are completely different, their friendship is often long-lasting. While they share some similar interests in dance, art, wine, and culture, a Taurus despises a Scorpio's evasions. Yet, this friendship is based on mutual respect and admiration for the opposite astrological sign, which is why it survives for a longer period. They continuously learn from each other. For instance, a Taurus appreciates a Scorpio's viewpoint and passion towards life, whereas a Scorpio wants to learn money management from a Taurus. For the friendship to last long, a Taurus must put up with a Scorpio's manipulation, and a Scorpio must ignore a Taurus' stubbornness.

Taurus and Sagittarius

While a Taurus is calculative and calm most of the time, a Sagittarius is extremely enthusiastic, which contradicts their natures. A Taurus monotony and ability to repeat things, outfits, and activities are puzzling to a Sagittarius. What's more, puzzling is their new and enthusiastic response to the same old activities. Even if you eat the same lunch every day, your excited reaction is mystifying to your Sagittarius friend. As a Taurus, if you need to incorporate some change in your life, you can always turn to a Sagittarius. But if a Sagittarius is looking for a light-hearted conversation or needs some cheering, they can ask their Taurus friend for help.

Taurus and Capricorn

These two are Earth signs, so they share similar traits, personalities, and aspirations. Even though you both are too picky, you bond quickly. This is because you understand the other's mindset and help them reach their goals. While a Capricorn yearns respect and stature, a Taurus adores and yearns beauty. Both need a comfortable and steady life. A Bull can help the Goat find a job, one they deserve, and put them in the spotlight. A major difference between these two signs is their working style and pattern. While a Capricorn works hard with no rest, a Taurus' laziness may be off-putting for them. Other than this, there is no serious reason for the friendship to weaken at any point.

Taurus and Aquarius

This friendship will be challenging for both signs. However, they know how to navigate their way through difficulties. Their interest and need for material possessions can often be a major difference between these signs, sometimes even a threat. While an Aquarius is least bothered about accumulating materials, a Taurus finds pleasure in it. Also, a Taurus prefers to be near his friends, whereas an Aquarius likes to be alone most of the time. However, since both signs appreciate each other for their strengths, this friendship can be enduring.

Taurus and Pisces

A friendship between these two signs is probably one of the easiest and light-hearted bonds among other pairings. Pisces possess a great sense of humor and creative skills, which a Taurus adores. But a Pisces admires a Taurus' practical approach and common sense. They both have something to offer in their friendship. For instance, a Pisces learns finance management and organizational skills from a Taurus, and a Taurus friend picks up creative skills from a Pisces. For the friendship to last long, a Taurus must put up with a Pisces' unpunctuality, and a Pisces must ignore a Taurus' inflexibility and stubbornness. To overcome these minor annoyances, find a hobby that you'd enjoy together.

Signs that Don't Get Along with Taurus

The complex interrelationships between the signs matter more than many people think. While it shouldn't be a deal-breaker, it should help you understand more why some of your relationships with friends or family are the way they are.

Taurus and Aries

Aries is one of the most active and competitive signs, making them often clash with Taurus. The definition of fun for both signs is different, which is why they usually have drastically contrasting interests. If they can cooperate to a greater extent, they can push each other to accomplish great goals. A Taurus can help Aries go through something that they rarely have the discipline to go through, while the Aries can open diverse paths that the Taurus was too conservative to approach.

Taurus and Gemini

Gemini doesn't have a long attention span, which usually results in them finding themselves in a million different things. This overwhelming divergence can cause them to stretch themselves too thin, which is the opposite of what a Taurus would do. Taurus appreciates familiarity and comfort zones, allowing them to focus on a single task or activity until they perfect it. They can both help each other out as one provides the other with different and useful perspectives.

Taurus and Sagittarius

The clash between Taurus and Sagittarius is basically about the unknown. Sagittarius thrives for tackling the unknown and unfamiliar territories. Taurus avoids the unknown and prefers to be surrounded with as much security as possible. This problem can become apparent in romantic relationships as their interests can create a big gap. Depending on the understanding of both parties, it is possible to find satisfying compromises.

Signs that Get Along with Taurus

Knowing which signs to look for can help you skip a lot of hassle. There is nothing wrong with looking for compatible signs that can make your life easier. Finding complementary signs can push you forward in your professional and social life.

Virgo and Taurus

Both Virgo and Taurus are earth signs, which means they have a high probability of enjoying each other's company. Both signs are known for their reliability and practicality, making them a great duo. A Taurus can provide enough stability to a Virgo to create a foundation that frequently allows the Virgo to push forward and reach its target. Having a Virgo as a friend or a partner is always a good idea as they are focused and provide matching energy.

Libra and Taurus

Earth and air-based signs are not usually the most compatible, but this rule may not directly apply to a duo composed of Libra and Taurus. It's believed that the Venus connection between the two signs makes them relatively stable. The emotional and subjective perspective of Taurus finds its polar opposite in the objective view of the Libra. They can match each other's tones and create a bridge that allows them to focus on what's important. These two signs are an excellent match for romantic and platonic relationships.

Pisces and Taurus

Earth and water are a great combination with the zodiac signs. The relationship between Pisces and Taurus is a dynamically synchronous one. Pisces complements the relationship with their devotion and idealism, while Taurus makes sure that they don't go off the grid with their realism. This can make a Pisces and Taurus duo quite powerful as they both can reduce the other's weaknesses. A loving relationship between the two can last for life, navigating problems as they go with great determination.

Taurus at a Party: Social Life

In this section, we will describe a party scene and see how the Taurus fits in.

If you are at a Taurus' birthday party or informal gathering, you are bound to have a blast. Since the Taurus has an eye for details, they are likely to throw a grand party to impress their guests. Also, since they're also major foodies and know their way in the kitchen, be ready to try delicious dishes at their party.

At someone else's party, a Taurus can be found meeting and talking to new people. They seem comfortable and are often seen with a drink (mostly a classy liquor type) in their hand. Even if they are in a corner, they seem to grab everyone's attention. They keep an eye on their close friends and make sure that they are fine. More important, they look out for their friends and make sure that they are not making a fool of themselves.

Why Does a Taurus Make a Great Friend?

Although a Taurus has many weaknesses, they are often minute and can be overlooked. Their strengths overpower their weaknesses, which makes them a loyal and reliable friend.

Here are five reasons friendship with a Taurus is valuable:

1. They Will Always Stay by Your Side

Even if you committed grave mistakes in your relationship, a Taurus believes in giving second chances. They will even help you correct your errors and get back on your feet. They are reliable and will always stay by your side. Also, if you desperately want to share a secret but not spread it further, you can rely on a Taurus, as they are secret bearers. They are loyal and will not spread gossip.

2. They Have a Solution to All Your Problems

Even if you mess up, your Taurus friend will have some solution to help you solve your issue. If you find yourself amid a crisis, call your Taurus friend up and let them help you. Even if you don't ask for help, they will do anything to make sure that your life is sorted. Whether it's an emotional family crisis or an intense project deadline, you can count on a Taurus to get you out of trouble. With a Taurus as a friend, your fridge is always loaded with beer, and your Netflix is paid every month.

3. They Oversee All Events

Whether it's your birthday or a school event, a Taurus will put their organizational skills into action and throw the best event one can imagine. Their impeccable management sense and attention to detail make them a valuable friend who can organize any event with little help. No wonder they make great managers. Even if it's your dog's birthday, they will always turn up with a doggie treat and candle.

4. They Will Show You the Better Side of Life

Due to their appreciation for food, art, culture, and luxury, they will guide you to life's finer things occasionally. With a Taurus friend, you can explore new restaurants and cuisines, take museum tours, or go wine tasting. This zodiac sign loves to eat and possesses a knack for cooking. With a Taurus as a friend, you will try new food and learn about the culinary world. Even if you can't afford to go out to a restaurant, a Taurus will whip up something delicious in their kitchen.

5. They Will Give You Expensive Presents

While this shouldn't be the sole reason to befriend a Taurus, it's an added benefit that not everyone is blessed with. A Taurus has expensive taste and prefers to use grand and luxurious material goods. Their clothes, shoes, bags, and gadgets are often high-end, and name brand. They not only want expensive things for themselves but also want their friends to experience luxury. Whether it's your birthday, graduation, or any other important event, your Taurus friend will always shower you with expensive gifts.

How to Foster a Taurus Friendship

As you can see, friendship with a Taurus is super valuable. However, their weaknesses can often get in the way and spoil your bond. To overcome this, go through these tips that will help you foster a Taurus friendship and sustain it for a long time.

How to Foster a Friendship Between a Taurus and Taurus

Even though both Taureans live through and understand their nature, certain aspects can clash and threaten their friendship. If you are a Taurus and want to sustain your friendship with a fellow Taurus, consider these tips:

1. Try to be More Understanding

The biggest problem that two Taureans can face in a friendship is a never-ending debate due to their stubbornness and argumentative nature. The only way to resolve this is to be more understanding. One or both Taurean friends must practice understanding, or it can cause a dent in their friendship. The first step is to listen. Instead of arguing and filling your head with a big "No" as they speak, listen to their viewpoint, and put yourself in their shoes. At times, they may have a point. The key is patience and an open mind.

2. Give Them Enough Time and Space When They are Angry

As Taureans friends, both of you may get easily angry and triggered due to your short tempers. If both of you get in a heated argument, give each other time instead of bombarding them with more viewpoints. Since a Taurus' temper dies down quickly, it is easier to resolve the issue when you give them enough time and space to think and contemplate the situation. Also, this zodiac sign despises drama in their life, which is why they resort to comfort and happiness after some time.

3. Make More Indoor Plans

If a Taurus earns money, they will likely spend it on a cozy home and luxurious material possessions. As a fellow Taurus, you too would prefer to stay indoors in your elegant home. To make plans with your Taurus friend, consider cooking together, watching a movie at home, ordering food, or getting a takeaway. Plans like these are more precious for two Taureans than to explore the outdoors. It will also give you enough time to learn about the other's whereabouts.

How to Foster a Friendship Between a Taurus and Other Zodiac Signs

As you learned through the friendship compatibility chart of a Taurus with other zodiac signs, a Taurus is a loyal and reliable friend. Though, certain negative aspects portrayed by other zodiac signs could affect their friendship with a Taurus. Here are three ways to maintain and foster a friendship with a Taurus:

1. It's All About Persistence

Since a Taurus is stubborn and wants things to go their way, the only solution to overcome similar situations is persistence. It is difficult to deviate from their plan and timetable. If you want a Taurus to follow your way without offending them, be persistent and polite simultaneously. Mention your desire occasionally. Even though they are stubborn, they will listen to you because this zodiac sign values friendship. At one point, they will realize the importance of putting their foot down and following their friend's wishes. Even if they say no to the first offer, keep insisting. They will eventually let their guard down and let you have your way.

2. Pay Attention to Important Dates

Taurus values important events and dates in their life. If you forget their birthday, graduation, anniversary, or other significant events, it may be difficult for them to forgive you. Every detail in a Taurus' life is important to them. So, as their friend, it should be important to you. To remember important dates, mark them on the calendar or set phone reminders. Celebrate with them instead of just congratulating or greeting them for the occasion. This is enough to make them happy and retain their loyalty.

3. Be Honest

A Taurus is an honest friend and expects you to be sincere. If they catch you lying or cheating, they will never forgive you. They may even break their friendship. Losing a Taurus in your life means losing an honest, loyal, and reliable friend, which is a rare kind. Even if the truth sounds bitter, never lie to a Taurus as they can easily decipher the difference. Due to their suspicious nature, they may cross-question your intentions too. They also hate it when someone gives a fake compliment. Dishonest flattery is off the charts. Be honest, even if it may offend them because it is better than lying and losing them forever.

A Taurus is a loyal and reliable friend who will show you the brighter side of life. Once you learn to put up with their stubbornness and laziness, they have a lot to offer. Their resilience and management skills are a lesson to be learned.

Appreciating Yourself as a Taurus

It's common for Taurus people to sell themselves short. This is to be expected from a sign that always shoots for the best and never retaliates until it gets what it wants. A Taurus needs to look at how far they've come and appreciated the progress that they've put. They are quite envied thanks to the effort and dedication they put into their lives. The discipline and responsibility needed to move on in life properly is something that Taurus has an abundance of. You can't expect people to respect your achievements if you don't respect them yourself.

It's time to look at success as a curve that's composed of a series of learning steps that you are gradually climbing. Don't expect that you must invent everything from scratch to be successful. You've already accomplished a lot, and it's never a good idea to think of the hard lessons you've endured as something to be swept away in disregard.

One problem that Taurus people struggle against is their attachment to the material world. A lot of the world's wealthiest people are Taurus signs. When you're dealing with low self-esteem problems, stop for a second and look at what you own, whether it's a Mercedes or a great career. Enjoying the luxuries you've collected over a long time is bound to make you understand that you're doing more than okay.

Just like any sign, Taurus has its merits and flaws. But a relationship with a Taurus will always be a great one.

A zodiac sign that aligns with Venus, the goddess of love, is going to be a strong advocate for big romantic gestures. The Taurus's love for ensuring that everything is planned and perfect makes them take quite a long time to get into a romantic relationship. They aren't just looking for any relationship, but the one. You'll always find their partners amazing because they are only attracted to the best. If you're in the early stages of dating a Taurus, you may find it difficult to catch their full and undivided attention, but once they choose you back, they will show a great level of genuine loyalty for a long time. If you happen to be the Taurus, you might want to take it easy when it comes to looking for perfection and try to enjoy people as they come with their good and bad.

Being a friend of a Taurus comes with its benefits, such as being trustworthy and loyal, but it's also important to know how to handle a Taurus's constant search for perfection. They may find it hard sometimes to match their standards, especially with sure signs like Aries, who can get very competitive. Fortunately, Taurus prefers to always go with the truth, so you don't have to keep an eye out for malicious lies or backstabbing.

Conclusion

As you finally start to understand your needs, complementary signs, and many other things about your sign, it becomes time to put it into action. You'll want to review your points of strength and weakness as a Taurus and see how you can improve them.

If you have a Taurus friend, count yourself lucky. There are a lot of great benefits you can enjoy due to the Taurus's nature and little quirks. While many people may be under the wrong impression with their temper, there are many things they might not know.

If you are a Taurus, expect most of your friends to come running to you for advice, whether it's about something romantic or a career decision. If there is one sign that's almost officially licensed to advise others, it will probably be Taurus. Common sense is their strongest ally, so is their ability to interpret situations on the move and multitasking. Separating emotions from individual situations allows them to see the problem from a vantage point. This gives them a more conclusive perspective. Making use of pros and cons lists is an excellent way for a Taurus to analyze almost any situation systematically. If emotions are running high, and the situation is getting out of hand, a Taurus can keep you grounded in common sense and logical thinking.

The Taurus is known to be one immovable rock when it comes to their preferences in friends and lovers. Many signs may switch partners or friends fast, but the Taurus sticks to their choices once they fixate their eyes on someone. They are looking for a way to enjoy the most out of what life offers, and that is done by keeping a balanced routine that builds their relationships upon love and trust. They are great friends you want to have your back in good and bad times.

A Taurus is actively interested in keeping their loved ones protected at all costs. They enjoy it rather than thinking of it as a chore like many other signs. A Taurus knows how to avoid making someone uncomfortable or uneasy, whether it's by giving him or her space or providing him or her with what they need. They have no problems taking on others' burdens, even if it means they must carry it all alone.

If you have a Taurus friend, you can expect to witness the finest things in life in multiple areas. Whether it's great music or obscure restaurants no one has heard of, they will travel to the ends of the earth to find something truly fitting to their taste. They also can appreciate almost everything and give it its fair share of thinking, which is one merit of being logical thinkers.

The perfectionism that a Taurus has whenever they are trying to improve themselves, or their work is simply inspiring. Having a Taurus friend can influence you to reach beyond what's at your fingertips. They are quite popular for their sense of self-control and ability to curb their appetite for activities that may stall their professional or artistic life. They simply find it uncomfortable to not be the best at what they do.

Creativity, love, stability, and aptitude are all great qualities of those born under the Taurus sign. Taurus' are a great gift to the universe, and we are blessed to have them in them in our lives.

Here's another book by Mari Silva that you might like

Your Free Gift (only available for a limited time)

Thanks for getting this book! If you want to learn more about various spirituality topics, then join Mari Silva's community and get a free guided meditation MP3 for awakening your third eye. This guided meditation mp3 is designed to open and strengthen ones third eye so you can experience a higher state of consciousness. Simply visit the link below the image to get started.

https://spiritualityspot.com/meditation

References

If You Are a Taurus, These Jobs Are Perfect for You ... (2017, July 12). Allwomenstalk.

https://money.allwomenstalk.com/if-you-are-a-taurus-these-jobs-are-perfect-for-you/7/

5 Ways To Overcome Your Fear Of Change During Tough Times. (2017, March 13). Molly Fletcher.

https://mollyfletcher.com/fear-of-change/

7 traits common to the strong-minded Taurus in your life. (2018, April 23). Well+Good.

https://www.wellandgood.com/taurus-personality-trait-gifs/

12 Astrology Zodiac Signs Dates, Meanings and Compatibility. (2010). Astrology-Zodiac-Signs.com.

https://www.astrology-zodiac-signs.com/

About Taurus the Bull: Astrology/Zodiac. (n.d.). Cafeastrology.com. Retrieved from

https://cafeastrology.com/zodiactaurus.html

All About Astrology: Zodiac Signs, the Planets, and Compatibility. (n.d.). Tarot.com. https://www.tarot.com/astrology

astrologer, M. H. M. H. is an, Reader, T., & Hall, author of "Astrology: A. C. I. G. to the Z. " our editorial process M. (n.d.). What are the Modalities? Cardinal, Fixed, Mutable. LiveAbout. Retrieved from https://www.liveabout.com/modalities-cardinal-fixed-or-mutable-206736

Astrologer, P. L. C. H. (n.d.). Taurus Weaknesses in Love and Relationships. LoveToKnow. Retrieved from https://horoscopes.lovetoknow.com/astrology-signs-personality/taurus-weaknesses-love-relationships

AstroTwins, T. (2017, August 6). Taurus Love Chart. ELLE. https://www.elle.com/horoscopes/love/a2231/taurus-compatibility/

Be Mine: Dealing With Possessiveness in a Relationship. (n.d.). Psychology Today. Retrieved from https://www.psychologytoday.com/us/blog/compassion-matters/201702/be-mine-dealing-possessiveness-in-relationship

Bozec, R. P., Jean-Pierre Nicola, Julien Rouger, Franck Le. (n.d.). Taurus-Scorpio: similarities and differences. Www.Astroariana.com. Retrieved from http://www.astroariana.com/Taurus-Scorpio-similarities-and.html

Compatible-Astrology.com. (n.d.). Taurus compatibility. Www.compatible-Astrology.com. Retrieved from https://www.compatible-astrology.com/taurus-compatibility.html

Constella, M. (2019, March 5). 9 Best Jobs for Taurus: Ideal Careers for Taurus Men & Women | Horoscope &

Astrology. Metropolitan Girls. https://metropolitangirls.com/best-jobs-taurus/

Cosmopolitan.com - The Women's Magazine for Fashion, Sex Advice, Dating Tips, and Celebrity News. (n.d.).

Cosmopolitan. https://www.cosmopolitan.com

Find the Best Career for Your Zodiac Sign - Taurus | ZipRecruiter®. (2019, May 7). ZipRecruiter.

https://www.ziprecruiter.com/blog/best-career-paths-taurus/

Free Taurus Kid Horoscope by The AstroTwins. (n.d.). Astrostyle: Astrology and Daily, Weekly, Monthly Horoscopes by The AstroTwins. Retrieved from https://astrostyle.com/family-horoscopes/baby-and-childrens-horoscopes/the-taurus-child/

How to Deal with a Taurus Partner's Stubbornness. (n.d.). The Femme Oasis. Retrieved from https://www.thefemmeoasis.com/astrology-zodiac/how-to-deal-with-a-taurus-partners-stubbornness/000007cc

How to Parent a Taurus. (n.d.). Www.Maisonette.com. Retrieved from https://www.maisonette.com/le_scoop/how-to-parent-a-taurus

Mom365. (2020). 8 Things to Know About Your Taurus Child. Mom365.com.

https://www.mom365.com/mom/astrology/all-about-your-taurus-childs-astrology

My Taurus Zodiac Sign: Love. (n.d.). Www.Horoscope.com. Retrieved from https://www.horoscope.com/zodiac-signs/taurus/love

PowerofPositivity. (n.d.). Power of Positivity: #1 Positive Thinking & Self Help Community. Power of Positivity: Positive Thinking & Attitude. Retrieved from https://www.powerofpositivity.com/

Rainer, M. A. (n.d.). Raising a Taurus baby? Find out the traits and challenges you may face. Www.Kidspot.com.Au. Retrieved from https://www.kidspot.com.au/parenting/parenthood/parenting-style/raising-a-taurus-baby-find-out-the-traits-and-challenges-you-may-face/news-story/0679dec1eec89d1fa8cf997dcd386b02

Taurus and their Personality and Physical Traits. (n.d.). Pointastrology.com.

Taurus Child: Personality Traits and Characteristics | Taurus Baby. (2018, September 22). ZodiacSigns-Horoscope.com. https://www.zodiacsigns-horoscope.com/taurus/taurus-child-traits-personality/

Taurus Friends & Family – Zodiac Signs. (n.d.). Retrieved from https://www.bzodiac.com/zodiac-signs/taurus-zodiac-sign/taurus-friends-family/

Taurus in Love - Sign Compatibility. (n.d.). The Love Queen. Retrieved from https://www.thelovequeen.com/taurus-love-horoscope-sign-compatibility/

Taurus Personality Traits, Characteristic, Strengths and Weaknesses. (n.d.). Your Zodiac Sign. Retrieved from https://www.yourzodiacsign.com/taurus/personality/

Taurus, Taurus Hobbies, Hobbies for taurus sign. (n.d.). Taurus.Findyourfate.com. Retrieved from

https://taurus.findyourfate.com/hobbies.html

Taurus Traits-Positive and Negative Characteristics. (2016). GaneshaSpeaks.

https://www.ganeshaspeaks.com/zodiac-signs/taurus/traits/

Taurus Weaknesses: Know Them so You Can Defeat Them. (2018, November 11). I.TheHoroscope.Co.

https://i.thehoroscope.co/taurus-weaknesses-know-them-so-you-can-defeat-them/

The Taurus Child: Taurus Girl & Boy Traits & Personality | Zodiac Signs for Kids. (n.d.).

Www.Buildingbeautifulsouls.com. Retrieved from https://www.buildingbeautifulsouls.com/zodiac-signs/zodiac-signs-kids/taurus-child-personality-traits-characteristics/

The Zodiac Sign Taurus Symbol - Personality, Strengths, Weaknesses. (2018, February 5). Labyrinthos. https://labyrinthos.co/blogs/astrology-horoscope-zodiac-signs/the-zodiac-sign-taurus-symbol-personality-strengths-weaknesses

Things You Should Know About a Taurus Child. (n.d.). Parenting.Firstcry.com. Retrieved from https://parenting.firstcry.com/articles/things-you-should-know-about-a-taurus-child/

Thinnes, C. (n.d.). Taurus Compatibility - Best and Worst Matches. Numerologysign.com. Retrieved from https://numerologysign.com/astrology/zodiac/compatibility/taurus-compatibility/

Waits, P. (2020, July 14). You Can Now Read the Four Best Professions for Taurus. Themagichoroscope.com. https://themagichoroscope.com/zodiac/best-jobs-taurus

What Sun Signs Say about Work Abilities: Taurus | News | Nexxt. (n.d.). Www.Nexxt.com. Retrieved from https://www.nexxt.com/articles/what-sun-signs-say-about-work-abilities-taurus-10871-article.html

Which Star Signs is Taurus Most Compatible With? (n.d.). AstroReveal. Retrieved from https://www.astroreveal.com/Which-Star-Signs-Should-You-Date.aspx?a=TAU

YourTango | Smart Talk About Love. (n.d.). Www.Yourtango.com. https://www.yourtango.com

Printed in Great Britain
by Amazon